From *Despair* to *Victory*

a true story

60 Exciting Years in the Ministry

From *Despair* to *Victory*

Dr. Ben Bates

Pleasant Word
A Division of WinePress Group
PW

Pleasant Word (a division of WinePress Publishing, PO Box 428, Enumclaw, WA 98022) functions only as book publisher. As such, the ultimate design, content, editorial accuracy, and views expressed or implied in this work are those of the author.

Unless otherwise noted, all Scriptures are taken from the *Holy Bible, New International Version®, NIV®*. Copyright © 1973, 1978, 1984 by the International Bible Society. Used by permission of Zondervan. All rights reserved.

Scripture references marked KJV are taken from the *King James Version* of the Bible.

Scripture references marked NASB are taken from the *New American Standard Bible,* © 1960, 1963, 1968, 1971, 1972, 1973, 1975, 1977 by The Lockman Foundation. Used by permission.

ISBN 13: 978-1-4141-1283-1
ISBN 10: 1-4141-1283-1
Library of Congress Catalog Card Number: 2008907119

I PROUDLY, AND with honor, dedicate my memoirs to my wife, Bettie; my son, Carey Franklin; my daughter, Donelia (Dodie) Bates (Davis); my son-in-law, Walter H. Davis; my daughter-in-law, Lynne Bates; my precious six grandchildren, Beth Ann (Davis) Bard, Heather Irene Bates, Hollie Gabriélle Bates, Walter H. Davis Jr., Bettie Dianne (Davis) Mayhew, and Hudson M. Bates; and to many precious friends who have blessed my life throughout these past 60 years. May God bless you.

Contents

Foreword
by Dr. John Sullivan

A RIVER FORMS as many tributaries flow into it. These smaller bodies of water converge together to produce a rushing river. Dr. Ben Bates has demonstrated this very principle in his memoir, *From Despair to Victory*.

Dr. Bates demonstrates great gifts of gratitude and recall in his exciting life story.

Beginning with humble beginnings and difficult times seems to always ready us for the long-run. Someone well said, "Life is not to be gulped—it is to be sipped." This enables us to enjoy the journey. No one comprehends this like a man called of God. Bates does not bemoan his humble beginnings; he allows this "tributary" to become one part of the river of his life. His meager beginnings were not a trial but a testimony.

So many people make so many contributions to our lives. However, no one makes a greater contribution than the preacher's wife. She becomes the counselor, disciplinarian, homemaker, "buffer zone," and loving critic—sometimes wrapped in an apron, and other times Sunday's best, but always on display. The attitude of the minister's wife constitutes the most significant and longest running "tributaries" into the man called of God. My observation about Dr. Ben, without Bettie, is that perhaps neither his life nor his ministry would have lasted 60 years!

Another "tributary" making the river of our life is the friends we make and the impact they have in shaping our lives. After family, friends shape us most. Charles and Judy Hill, Greg and Barbara Walcott, "Doc" Dishner, and various pastors all helped to form the valleys and peaks of Ben Bates' life and ministry. Gratitude for these friends breathes on every page.

There is no question that when you read this compelling story, you will look over your shoulder and remember many of those who helped form your life and ministry. When you do, let the words of Psalms 46:4 bless you, "There is a river, the streams whereof shall make glad the city of God..." (KJV). Ben Bates is one of the "rivers" that blesses God.

Dr. John Sullivan,
Executive Director-Treasurer
Florida Baptist Convention

Presenting a man you'll never forget!

AFTER READING THE events of the life of Dr. Ben Bates, as recorded in his book, I have been inspired by the way that God has used him in evangelism, in the pastorate, in denominational service, and in his influence for our Lord upon the lives of so many people. As a personal friend, I have known him for many years. I made my first acquaintance with him while pastoring the Park Avenue Baptist Church in Nashville, Tennessee, for thirty-five years. His daughter, Dodie, was married to one of our staff members, Walter Davis, and she was greatly loved by our membership and looked upon as one of our finest and sweetest members. I also had the privilege of being the pastor of Dr. Bates while he was employed in Nashville. This book will challenge you to be a greater personal witness for Christ, to remember that, as Christians, we all have times when we get knocked down, but we don't get knocked out, because our loving Lord places His arms around us, causing us to stand on our feet once more and to keep on being fruitful and faithful to Him. Dr. Bates also reminds us that at the end of this short journey called "life," the only important thing will be to hear Christ say, "Well done, good and faithful servant." May you be blessed by this book as I have been blessed.

Your fellow servant in Christ,
Pastor Bob Mowrey,
First Baptist Church, Scottsboro, TN
Pastor emeritus: Park Avenue Baptist Church,
Nashville, TN

Chapter 1

Early Years

IBEGIN MY memoirs, the story of my 60 years in the Lord's service, by giving some background of my life that began 84 years ago on June 5, 1924, in a poor, rural farming community in Lonoke County, Arkansas. I was born the first of five sons to Ben and Ellie Bates, a poor share-crop-farmer family, in a time of extreme poverty, when it was exceedingly difficult for two to make a living, let alone start a family.

Life expectancy in those days was less than 50 years. There were but a few automobiles in all of America. There was not more than a thousand miles of gravel and hard surfaced roads in all the state of Arkansas. The maximum speed of motorized vehicles was 40 miles per hour. The average hourly wage was 40 cents per hour. The average public worker made less than a thousand dollars annually. A farm day-worker made 50 to 75 cents a day, working from dawn to dark. And 90 percent of all births took place in the home bedroom with the assistance of a mid-wife.

Times were hard and difficult, and for my parents to eke out a livelihood; raise five boys; clothe, feed, and send them all to school; and literally climb out of the worst living conditions one can possibly imagine was a miracle in itself. The conditions of that day and time would be difficult to impossible for this generation to imagine. However, we never knew we were poor and poverty ridden, as we think of those conditions today, because everybody in our rural part of the country was in the same condition. Nevertheless, by very hard work and sheer determination, my mother and daddy always believed that there would come a brighter day if they worked hard and kept the faith and never gave up. Thank God, through great sacrifice, extreme difficulty, and back-breaking hard work, those better times eventually came.

Entire family in front of first new home in 1940

In 1938, through a government program to help poor farmers, my parents were able to move into a new home on a 40-acre tract of rich farmland near Scott, Arkansas. They were also given two mules with which to farm the land and 40 years to pay the debt. I was 14 years old, and for the first time since my parents were married, my daddy and mother and five brothers all had a decent home to live in. From that day forward, life began to change, but not without a lot of hard work.

When my daddy went home to be with the Lord, he left my mother with a comfortable farm home, 40 acres of farmland that was debt free, money enough in the bank, and all the necessities she needed to continue on for 17 more years, while living alone, before going home to be with the Lord at age 84.

When I remember my heritage and reflect on the long and difficult journey through which my parents traveled—the abject poverty and privation of those desperate times through the Depression years that I can remember so well—I have to humbly say that I owe every success and every accomplishment of my life to godly parents who made every effort to instill into their sons the very things that sustained them through the worst of times and the best of times.

When I was 16 years of age, I embraced my parents' faith and became a follower of the Lord Jesus Christ. I was converted in a small Baptist mission revival being held in a vacant store building on Broadway Street in North Little Rock, Arkansas, on the seventh day of July. I was baptized on July 14, 1940, in the Immanuel Baptist Church in Little Rock, Arkansas—the church that founded and sponsored the small mission.

Because I lived 18 miles away from the city, I moved my membership to the Toltec Baptist Church near the farm where my parents lived. For the next two years, I put forth every effort into walking and living the life of a believer, and I believed that I had made good progress. However, the United States was entering a time of war, and I wanted to choose a branch of service in which I could serve. I chose to enter the Navy in 1942 and was sent to San Diego, California, where I received my boot camp training. I had lived a sheltered country boy's life, and because of the Christian atmosphere of our home, I had not been exposed to the world. Before I knew what was happening, I began to indulge in things I never knew existed. Through the encouragement of my fellow servicemen, I began to experiment with alcohol. One thing led to another, and yet I could sense in my heart that this way of life was not right.

U S Navy, 1942, San Diego, CA

Ben in the Navy

Following eight weeks in boot-camp training, I was given a 10-day leave to return home. I had left behind someone who had become the love of my life. I had met Bettie Morgan while attending a New Year's Eve party in the home of the Morgan family in North Little Rock in 1940. We had dated each other for about 19 months, and though we were young—she was 18 and I was 19—we wanted to be married. While I was on my leave, we hurriedly got married and had five short days together before I had to return to my base in San Diego.

After several months, I managed to send for Bettie, and she came by train to Los Angeles, where we lived with her Aunt Annie and Uncle Ben Waddle until we could afford our own apartment. My 66-dollar monthly pay as an apprentice seaman badly needed supplementing in order for two to exist, so Bettie went to work for the Douglas Aircraft factory in Long Beach. Her salary made it possible for us to get our first apartment, but we could not afford a car, so all of our travel was by street bus or with friends or relatives.

By this stage in my life, I had drifted far away from where I had been when I entered the Navy. I was like the prodigal son of the Bible who had left home, gone away to a foreign country, and become involved in riotous living. I was living on "Fool's Mountain" and had been drawn away from the principles, standards, and parental training of the first 18 years of my life. Satan had taken control of my life, as he can so cleverly do, and was tearing down all that was good, decent, and wholesome.

The memory of that wilderness experience still shames and sorrows me to this day. Although every sin and stain has long since been removed, the memories of that time still linger and often are as bitter as wormwood. I have spent a lifetime reminding the young men and women whom I have seen drifting onto the wrong track of life to *"be not deceived,*

Ben and his new wife, Bettie

for God is not mocked, for whatsoever you sow, that you shall also reap" (Galatians 6:7 KJV).+ Sin bites like a serpent and stings like an adder.

I received a medical discharge from the Navy in 1945, after spending six months in the Naval Hospital at Corona, California. I had contracted tuberculosis, and therefore I could not return to active duty. This was one of my life's great disappointments. Being stationed on an air base, I had spent much of my spare time out on the flight line watching planes warm up and take off. I had a deep desire to fly an airplane, and I finally mustered up enough courage to ask some of the pilots if I could hitch a ride with them. That wasn't difficult at all. After many such rides—even getting to follow through on the flight controls during dive bombing runs and some of the dog fight maneuvers—some of the pilots began to encourage me to go for flight training. Some of them even put in a good word to flight command for me.

Their encouragement and belief in my abilities led me to put in a request to become a naval pilot. The thrill of my life came the day I was notified that my request had been granted and that I was to report to begin my physical. After passing all of the tests, I was taken off all duty and notified that I would be relocating to Pensacola, Florida, where I would receive my flight training. But all of this shattered a few days later, when I was diagnosed with tuberculosis. It was as if a bomb had exploded and taken my dreams and hopes of becoming a Navy pilot along with it. My career in the Navy was too short lived. After one year, 10 months, and 20 days, I was discharged back to civilian life.

Chapter 2

A New Beginning

A FTER MY DISCHARGE from the Navy, I returned home to Little Rock to resume civilian life. Shortly thereafter, I was given a traveling position with an advertising firm that paid me more money in one year than I had earned in the past several years put together. It was great to have more income, but this just served to pave the way for me to wander further from the Lord. God really had not gotten my attention, even after the health tragedy. I had forgotten a certain verse in the Bible: "Whatsoever a person sows that shall he also reap" (Galatians 6:7b KJV).

It was obvious that I was reaping a whirlwind and that my moral life was in shambles. Many of my friends, who loved me and saw the way that I was living, told me they were praying for me. In the deep of my heart, I knew that I belonged to the Lord Jesus. God wouldn't let me go without exerting great conviction! And truthfully, I knew that I was not happy and at peace with my life. I would come home at night, and in the still of the darkness, I would toss and turn and feel remorse and emptiness for the way my life was going. I knew fully well from my early childhood and the strong Christian example set by my parents that I was on a crash course. I knew in the deep of my soul that when I had found Christ on that hot July night in Little Rock, Arkansas, I had been bought with a price more precious than rubies and fine gold and that God had something planned for my life even before the foundation of the world.

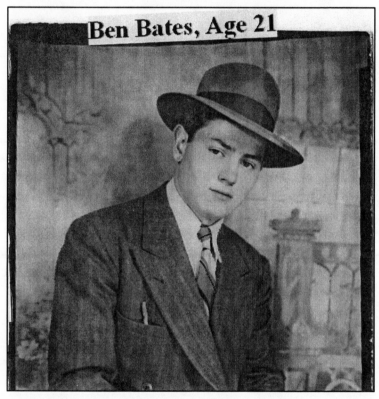

Ben Bates, Age 21

21-year-old Ben Bates, advertising salesman

Finally, it was as if the Lord firmly said, "This far, and NO farther!" I had drifted so far away from the transformed life of that 16-year-old boy back on the farm in 1940 and become so disillusioned that I even contemplated taking my own life. I had it all planned out and had placed a note in my pocket expressing my sorrow for the disappointment I had been. However, God had other plans for my life.

That Sunday afternoon, there was a young man passing out gospel tracts at Third and Main Street in downtown Little Rock. It so happened that as I passed by, the person reached out his hand and offered me a tract. I took the gospel tract and stopped to look at it. I was immediately startled by the headline: "STOP! Have You Considered Your Destiny?" I knew that I was at my extreme end of hope and that this was God's planned way of getting my attention. I read the tract, which seemed to have been written just for me at that moment in time.

Instead of walking three blocks east to the Main Street Bridge, where I had planned to jump, I changed direction and walked 10 blocks back to the First Baptist Church of Little Rock, located at Twelfth and Louisiana Street, where a large group of young people were getting ready to go into the worship service at about 7 o'clock. They called out to me as I approached and invited me to come join them. I went with them into the service. The house was packed, and I was very confused as I sat near the back of the auditorium. It seemed that every word the preacher spoke was especially for me. The longer I listened, the more conviction gripped my soul, and it seemed that I could hear a still, small voice saying, *This is where I have brought you to find an end to the sorrow and brokenness of your life.*

I found myself halfway down the long aisle when the invitation was given for those who wished to unite with the church and forsake the sin that had broken their fellowship with the Lord to come forward. There, I asked the pastor, Dr. R. C. Campbell, to help me as I asked the Lord for forgiveness and restoration from the journey that had led me deep into the wilderness. In my broken, weeping voice,

I told him, "Sir, I am far, far away from God, and my life is terribly messed up. I need help."

I left the First Baptist Church that evening with a sense of peace in my heart that I had not felt in years. I knew that God had fully forgiven me of my waywardness and sin and that a new and wonderful way of life was opening up for me. I had no idea of the things that God had in store for me after the rollercoaster life of turmoil and unrest that I had lived, but I was thankful that it was finally ending.

Bettie and I returned to Los Angeles, even to the same little two-room apartment where we had lived during my Navy days. Bettie had always been the strong believer. How I thank God for that! Bettie had many Christian relatives in the area who were members of the Florence Avenue Baptist Church. This was a new beginning for both of us. I had sought and received forgiveness from Bettie, friends, and family for the hurts and disappointments I had caused and for all those wasted years I had spent away from the Lord. I was eager for God to revitalize me and make me into the person He had planned for my life. I wanted what others whom I had begun to meet had in their lives.

God works in mysterious ways, His wonders to perform. There was never a doubt that what had happened to me on July 7, 1940, was real. God had never forsaken me. He was there all the time. It was I who had forsaken Him. He had always had a marvelous plan for my life, and I was beginning to rediscover the peace and contentment that had been missing in my life for all those wasted years.

Bettie and I both felt that we wanted to repeat the wedding vows we had originally made on November 17, 1942. Arrangements were made to have Reverend Ted Goodman, the pastor of the Florence Avenue Baptist Church (where most of Bettie's relatives attended), to officiate. We repeated our vows in the home of Bettie's Aunt Annie and Uncle

Ben Waddle. Our return to California had brought many new friends into our lives, and we were eager to establish ourselves in an environment where we could meet Christian friends who were deeply grounded in the faith. The Lord had certainly brought us to the right place for our spiritual life to grow and mature.

Bettie and I became members of the Florence Avenue Baptist Church and began attending services every Wednesday night and on Sunday. We made a number of interesting new friends with whom we grew very close in the faith. Soon, things began to happen in my life that I had never known or experienced before. God was beginning to do something especially wonderful in my life. I felt as if I had been given a spiritual bath and that every weight of sin had been taken away. I began to develop a deep longing and love for spiritual things. I began spending many hours reading and studying the Scriptures. I had a desperate love for and desire to serve the Lord, and for the first time in my life, being a Christian really *meant* something special to me.

I had always heard the saying, "Man's extremity is God's opportunity." Well, Bettie and I were two young people who you might say were just starting over. Although we had been married for several years, I had let Satan literally destroy what earthly possessions we owned. We had no automobile, no furniture, and no money...just the bare necessities of life. But even though we were down, we were not out!

Chapter 3

Called to Ministry

A T THIS POINT in our new beginning, Bettie went to work for Hormel Packing Company, and I found employment with Pep Boys automotive store, a business that still exists today. I worked as a sales clerk, a job I was familiar with given the fact that I had been employed with a similar company back in Arkansas.

My new commitment to the Lord Jesus had put a fire in me to tell others about my faith and what God had done for me. At lunchtime, I would quickly eat my sandwich, and with a pocket full of gospel tracts, I would take off down the street and pass out tracts to anyone who would stop for a moment and let me witness to them. I would present the Lord Jesus Christ, and there was hardly a day that I would not see one or more individuals accept the Lord Jesus as Savior. My fellow workers began to poke fun at me and call me "the preacher."

I had such a desire to see others come to my Savior that I would witness to customers in the store. However, the bosses were Jewish, and they sternly warned me that if I didn't stop harassing the customers about that "Jesus business," they were going to let me go. Taking this threat seriously, I became far more discrete about talking to customers while on duty, but I would still follow the customer to the door and give him or her a gospel tract as he or she was leaving. I learned that even this was not acceptable, and I was again warned that I must never speak to a customer about religious matters while on duty. I respected my bosses' rule. But it is evident from what happened after work one evening that they never trusted me to heed their warnings.

One Friday evening, at about 9 o'clock, I checked out my register and walked over to the door to leave. As my boss unlocked the door, he looked at me with a stern expression on his face and handed me an envelope that contained my last paycheck. "You are fired," he said. "I warned you about your religion and preaching Jesus to our customers while on duty." Frankly, I was shocked and saddened at the idea of having to go home to my wife and tell her I had been fired because I was telling people about Jesus and handing out gospel tracts. But I suddenly realized that this wasn't a bad reason for losing one's job.

I knew that we wouldn't go hungry. Bettie was employed by Hormel Packing Company, and every week or so she brought home bacon and tenderloin steak that she was able to buy at the employee's price. In those days, that price wasn't bad at all. We actually ate steak more often than we do now.

I wasn't unemployed but for a few days. The Lord soon led me to one of the largest automobile parts distributors in the Los Angeles area: Kay & Burbank Automotive. The company distributed automotive parts and equipment to the whole state of California and to all adjoining states— and even to South America. I started as a trainee and began to learn automotive parts and distribution. I was quickly moved into the department that received all the incoming orders for processing and shipment. I enjoyed my work, because I had freedom to talk to many employees about Jesus. I even got to share Christ with the executives with no fear of being dismissed. Lunchtime was a favorite part of the workday, because it was easy for me to talk with different people about Jesus, read my New Testament, and pass out tracts.

One time, the owner and three of the top executives of the company asked me to accompany them to a meeting at one of the large convention centers, where they would be exhibiting our products. There, I would meet buyers from several foreign countries who were potential customers for our products. I was honored to be asked, but I had no idea what my involvement would be—and I didn't think to ask. When we arrived early that afternoon, I was asked to assist in serving the alcoholic drinks. This meant that I would be serving hard liquor, wine, and beer. I asked the president of the company if I could have a personal word with him. I said, "Sir, you are asking me to do something that my convictions as a Christian will not permit me to take part in. Is there something else I can do to show my respect for you and our company?" The president looked at me and said, "There is a soft drink area over there that you may take charge of." I later explained my convictions concerning the matter to my superiors, and through the episode I was able to give a strong testimony of my faith.

God was working in so many ways in my life as He prepared me for what He had in store. I was eager to learn everything I could about the work of the Lord. I couldn't wait to get off from work and join the "band of brothers" I had bonded with from the Florence Avenue Baptist Church. Being more seasoned Christians, they were a tremendous help to me in my new life. Our favorite ways to minister were witnessing, conduction street meetings, and passing out gospel tracts. We also spent time studying the Bible.

One evening, when we were walking the street and passing out gospel tracts, I passed a bar and suddenly felt the Holy Spirit speak to me to go into the bar and give out tracts. I obeyed and went in. The bar was dimly lit and smoked-filled and packed with customers. I asked the owner if I could have permission to give gospel tracts to the customers. To my shock, he granted permission. So I began going around to the tables giving out tracts. One of the customers loudly protested to the owner and asked that I be thrown out. The owner shouted back over the noise of the jukebox and loud talking, "Go on about your business. The young man is not hurting anybody, and besides, some of you bums need to read what he has given you."

That was an unforgettable experience. When I came out of the bar after a few minutes, one of the guys from the church saw me and asked me what I was doing in there. I explained to him that there were many lost men and women in the bar and that God had told me to give them all a tract and witness to them. I felt that I had broken a barrier and found a great place to witness, and it wasn't the last time I went into a bar to witness for my Lord. The Pharisees accused Jesus of being a friend of sinners and eating with them. I didn't eat or drink with them, but I did shake some hands, and I even received a thank you from a few of them.

It is amazing how quickly my five new friends and I bonded in the Lord. After all these years, some of those experiences we had together are as fresh as if they happened yesterday. These five men—Paul Walker, Malcolm (Doc) Dishner, Jasper Burdett, Basel Huett, and Bill (a very sharp Bible student from the Bible Institute of Los Angeles [BIOLA], whose last name I cannot recall)—and I became closer than most brothers in the flesh. They came into my life at a time when I needed encouragement and spiritual guidance. The six of us would meet for Bible study and prayer at least two times each week in a special little room at the church. Oftentimes, we would go there even on a Sunday morning and get on our knees and pray during the entire service—especially when our pastor, Reverend Ted Goodman, was preaching. During one such time, it turned out to be the prayer meeting of my life.

The six of us met one evening about 7 o'clock for what we thought would be just another prayer meeting and Bible study. At first, there was nothing unusual about the meeting. But as the evening passed, God seemed to be present in an indescribable way. We became so engaged in what the Lord was doing that we were totally oblivious of time. The sun rose the next morning before we realized that the night had past. Never before had any of us experienced the unspeakable presence of the Lord as we did that night. That single night became a life-changing experience for me. I shall never forget how the presence of God was as real as if He were literally there in person. I believe He was!

The next Sunday, a guest preacher was speaking at our church. Bettie and I arrived a few minutes late that morning and had to sit far back in the rear of the auditorium. My soul was burning within me to make some kind of open commitment to the Lord, though I had not yet discussed this with Bettie or anyone else—not even my "band of brothers." I had known for months that the Holy Spirit was tugging at me strongly to surrender to Him and commit to some type of full-time Christian ministry. I had often had the urge to make that decision at other times, but I just couldn't seem to bring myself to do it.

As the guest preacher spoke that morning, I felt the most compelling urge I had ever experienced to surrender my mind, body, and soul to serve the Lord in some kind of full-time Christian work. Exactly what that work was, I was not sure. It seemed as if the preacher would go on and on and never stop and give the invitation. Finally, Pastor Goodman said, "Let's stand and sing our hymn of invitation. And if God is speaking to someone today to make a decision, will you come on this first verse?" Ten strong men could not have held me back that morning. I don't know whether I ran down the aisle or walked briskly or how I made it down there. All I know is that brother Goodman met me and said, "Benny [that was the given name I went by at that time], why are you coming?"

I felt all of my strength ebb out of me at that the moment, and I fell upon my knees at the altar and sobbed out my commitment to the pastor and the Lord. I can still hear myself saying the words: "Lord, Jesus, I surrender all my life to You upon my knees to preach or be a missionary or do anything You want me to do. From this day forth, I will be at Your command and wish." I felt someone kneel by my side. It was Bettie. She said, "Whatever God is calling you to do, I surrender my life with you."

The house was filled. The pastor prayed with me, and when the service ended, he announced to the people that I had surrendered my life for "full-time Christian service." It seemed like everybody in the church came by and hugged me and wept with me and rejoiced that God had done such a mighty thing in my life. My five prayer buddies all waited until everyone had wished me God's blessings, and then one by one they hugged me and wept with me and rejoiced. I recall one of them—I believe it was Basel—saying, "We have been waiting for this day to come in your life. We knew it was coming."

God had minutely woven my life and being into what He had planned for me for years to come. I was beginning to see what God could do with a life that was yielded to Him. Although I did not know what He had in store for me, I knew for the first time that He had called me to a special ministry and that He would reveal that ministry to me in His own time.

Chapter 4

Sermon at the Mission

MY BAND OF brothers had a mission ministry they served at four Monday evenings of each month in one of the rescue missions in the Long Beach and the San Pedro areas. They would load up in someone's car on a Monday evening at about 5 o'clock and take off for one of the rescue missions, where one of the men would take his turn in bringing the main message at 7 o'clock. Each of the men took turns bringing the message each week. I had been going along and having the time of my life as I witnessed to the men at the mission and served at the invitation time. I loved to mix with the crowd after the service and tell different men how wonderful it was to be a believer. And I also enjoyed giving my personal testimony.

I will *never* forget what happened on the way home after one of these services. God had worked in a mighty way, and we were rejoicing at how the Holy Spirit had worked to save several souls that night. Then, out of the blue, one of the fellows said, "Benny, next Monday night will be your night to bring the message at the San Pedro Rescue Mission." I was never known to be at a loss for something to say, but at that moment, I couldn't say a word. I believe it was Basel Huett who said, "Now that God has called you to full-time service—and since next Monday night will be your first time to give your testimony—maybe God wants you to be a preacher." When I finally gained my composure, I said, "Men, I've never done this before." I believe the whole gang said in unison: "Well, you've got six days to get your first sermon, for you are next!" I suppose you could say I was railroaded into preaching my first sermon by five of the dearest friends I ever had.

At this time in our life, Bettie and I had saved enough money to relocate to a larger and nicer apartment with a kitchen, living room, bedroom, and bath. It was like moving into a new world. The grounds were beautifully kept by a gardener. The apartments were rather new and excellently maintained. Some of our church friends lived in the apartments, and our friendship and fellowship with them grew even stronger. Life was getting better, and Bettie and I were both growing in the Lord.

When I came home that evening, all I could think about was, *What on earth will I talk about?* At that point in time, I didn't refer to the message I would be delivering as a "sermon." To be honest, I was scared beyond any words I could find to describe my feelings. On the other hand, I knew that the Lord would help me put together a message for that crowd of men at the mission. Although I had given my life to Him for full-time Christian service, I was still not exactly sure what He wanted me to do with my life.

In my childhood days, I had some passing thoughts about going to Africa and becoming a missionary (I will discuss one particular ministry experience I had while visiting the southern Baptist mission fields in Africa in a later chapter). I remember that when I was a small child, I would carry the water bucket to the hired workers in the field as they picked cotton. I must have been six years old. There would be 10 to 15 blacks singing as they worked their way down the cotton rows. I vividly recall climbing up on the stump of a sawed-off tree in the cotton field and preaching to the hired workers as they picked cotton. One dear and blessed black lady, "Aunt Sally," was loved by our family. She was a very religious person, and I can still hear her slap her hands on her hips and say, "My Lord, that boy is going to be a preacher when he grows up, yes he is." How I praise the Lord that the prophesy of that precious lady came true in 1948.

Arriving home that evening, I told Bettie that the men had said that I would be giving my testimony the next Monday night at the mission in San Pedro. That meant that I would actually be preaching a sermon. I had no idea how preachers got their sermons. I just supposed that they prayed a lot and read their Bible a lot and God would impress them to speak on something. Then they would just get up and open their mouth, and God would fill it. I actually did it in the way I just described. I opened my Bible to Matthew 7:7–11 and studied and thought about those verses. And I certainly did a lot of praying.

It was a miracle, for out of those verses God gave me a sermon. I wrote it all out and then stood before the full-length mirror in our living room. Over and over again, I looked into that mirror and imagined a crowd of lost people as I delivered my sermon. I would preach aloud as a dying man would if it were the last sermon he would ever preach, although it was only to be my first. I prayed a lot and told God that I was afraid and needed His help. And did God come through? I should say He did. He always does—and has for these 60 years.

From Despair to Victory

As we traveled to the mission late that afternoon, I was very quiet and didn't do much talking. Pastor Goodman and Bettie went with us that evening. The mission was always packed with every kind of sinner you can imagine, and there must have been 200 or more men in the meeting place that night. This was a normal crowd, because the men always got something to eat, and most of them got a bed for the night. I had a captive audience.

The men liked to sing. They didn't always sing on key, nor was their melody always in unison, but they sang loudly. When it was time for me to preach, I felt much like King Belshazzar in the Bible, whose knees smote one against the other when he saw the hand writing on the wall. My knees were like Jell-O those first few minutes. But then I looked out and saw my band of brothers, my pastor, and my wife all sitting there, and I knew they were praying for me. I got a super lift from the Holy Spirit, and for the next 25 minutes I preached to the crowd. To this day I couldn't tell you what I said, or if I said anything I had planned to say, but when I gave the invitation, I was soaking wet with perspiration. When I asked that all heads be bowed for prayer, I prayed for souls to be saved. After a few moments of prayer and asking sinners to repent and come to the front if they wanted Christ to become their Savior, seven men responded to accept the Lord Jesus Christ.

After the service, I happened to get the chance to talk with one of these men. This man was special, and he told me a story I shall never forget. He said that once upon a time he was very rich and owned one of the largest bridge building construction companies in California. In fact, he said that it was his company that had won the contract for building the Golden Gate Bridge in San Francisco. However, shortly afterward, he divorced his wife, gave up his family, and was later convicted of a crime that sent him to prison

26

for 25 years. When he got out of prison, he became a skid row drunken bum. "And now," he said to me, "I am an old man."

I remember putting my arm around him and saying, "Was what happened down there a while ago real, or was it a lie?" With tears in his eyes and a sob in his voice, he said, "It was the most real thing that has happened to me in my entire life." Only God knows what the end result of that man's decision that night turned out to be. The results belong only to the Lord Jesus!

We loaded up to make the journey back to Los Angeles, and on the way back, Bettie asked Pastor Goodman, "Pastor, how long do you think it will be before Benny can start preaching?" Brother Goodman said, "Start? He started tonight." If I had ever had a doubt about God's call on my life and what that call was, I now knew for certain. I have never since doubted His call on my life to *evangelism*.

Chapter 5

Seminary Life

M Y BAND OF brothers started calling me their "preacher," though I didn't feel like one. I was totally without knowledge as to the life of a preacher, my training for the ministry had not officially begun, and I was not even licensed or ordained. I considered myself a layman.

A few days went by. One Sunday morning, when Bettie and I were leaving the church following a morning worship service, Brother Goodman put his hand on my shoulder and said, "Are you ready to preach your first sermon in our church?" With astonishment written all over my face, I pointed to the pulpit up front and said, "Pastor, do you mean you want me to preach from up *there*?" With a big smile on his face, Pastor Goodman said, "How about, say, three Sunday evenings from now?"

Once again, I went through my wild method of preparing a sermon, standing before a full-length mirror and imagining that crowd of several hundred people sitting out there. I have truly forgotten what the subject of my sermon was, but I do remember that I was frightened half to death. I wondered what I could say to these several hundred people who knew me and had just witnessed my surrendering my life to be a preacher a few weeks before. I think I prayed that it would rain and storm that night so the crowd would be smaller. But no such luck. Maybe the people came out of curiosity to hear one of their own young men and see what God had to work with, but the house was packed.

I don't have to tell you I was nervous. I have preached no telling how many times to very small and very large crowds throughout my 60 years, but I still can't get over those first few moments of tenseness and nervousness when I step up to the pulpit to serve my precious Lord. I have gotten used to that feeling, and I pray I shall always have it. Without that feeling of utter dependency, I might be tempted to think, *Lord, I can do it all by myself.*

I didn't time myself that evening, but I am told the sermon lasted 30 minutes. As I faced that crowd of friends and visitors, I expressed my fear and asked them to pray for me. I remember saying, "I know my five prayer buddies are in the little room out back praying for me, and I know God is going to be honored and get the glory, so will you join me in prayer before I begin my sermon?" From that point forward, I can't recall anything of what I said. I don't even remember the text or subject of my sermon. How I wish I had kept that one for the record—I'm sure it would not have made it into the sermon hall of fame! However, I do remember that when the invitation was given, the entire front of the auditorium was filled with people responding to the call for some reason or another. It was a hallelujah time in the old meeting house after the service that night.

People hugged me, told me they would be praying for me, and assured me of God's call on my life. As the service ended, the pastor asked everyone to be seated. He asked me to stand with him at the pulpit. Then he reached under the pulpit, pulled out a piece of paper, and said, "The Florence Avenue Baptist Church, with great pleasure and honor, wishes to extend to you, Benny Bates, our fullest blessings, and promise to you our faithful prayers by giving you this official license that signifies we have put our approval upon your ministry." It grieves me to tell you that at some point over the years I lost that important document that set me apart to preach the Word.

I was still working with the large automotive company at that time. However, I had made request to be accepted as a student at the California Baptist Seminary, which was located in Los Angeles. I soon received word that I had been accepted and would begin classes the next semester, which was only a few weeks off. I resigned from my job and became a full-time student. Fortunately, having served in the military, I was eligible for the G.I. bill, which would pay for all my education expenses.

By the time I finished my first semester in seminary, I had received invitations to preach at four revivals in and around the Los Angeles area. By the time I was halfway through my second semester, I had visited every rescue mission in downtown Los Angeles, introduced myself to each one, and told the people there that I was a preaching student at California Baptist Seminary. I impressed on the director of each mission that if one of their noon-day speakers should have to cancel, they could call the president's office at the seminary and, even if I were in class, I could be at their mission and ready to preach within 10 to 20 minutes. I told the director of each mission that I was young and a fast runner and that I could get to any one of the four missions in less than 20 minutes. I could easily be there before the singing was over. I wanted to preach!

I bought a box of Scripture cards and began memorizing them. That really helped me to get started. There was hardly a week that passed that I didn't receive a call from one of the four missions. Many times a call would come when I was in class, but the president, Dr. John Bunyan Smith, would always allow me to go. Many were the times that I ran 20 or more blocks and arrived at a mission just in time to step in the pulpit and begin my message. One of the wonderful things was that each of the missions had Scripture passages printed on all the walls in large letters for the men to read. I would actually run my eyes around those walls, lift out various verses, and build my sermon on those passages as though I had planned to use them all along. And did the men listen? Yes! During the time I was in seminary, I saw literally hundreds of lives that had been shipwrecked on the beach of time come to Jesus and anchor their souls in His haven of rest.

At this early stage of my ministry, I was not knowledge-able about a great many things. For instance, I knew little to nothing about counseling, being a pastor of a church, conducting a worship service, marrying people, or conduct-ing a funeral. The fact of the matter was that I had not given much thought to any of these things. However, when I had been in seminary for only a little more than a couple of semesters, I suddenly found myself confronted with an invitation to perform a wedding.

My wife's cousin, Carolyn Barnwell, asked me to perform her wedding ceremony. Although I had never married anyone before, I thought this would be a great opportunity to get started. It would be a first for Carolyn and Tom, the young man she had chosen to be her partner for life, and a first for me. I felt rather calm about doing the wedding, until Carolyn told me that they were going to be married at the Los Angeles Youth for Christ rally being held on a Saturday night. I had been attending those rallies and knew that several thousand people customarily attended them.

I must have turned as white as a ghost with shock when I heard the news.

Carolyn and Tom's wedding

The first thought that entered my mind was, *Remember how you felt when your band of brothers told you that you would be giving your testimony at the rescue mission? Or again when you were asked to preach your first sermon in the church where you were a member? Well, here you go again.* Here I was facing my first wedding—which would take place before some 3,000 people—and I had no idea how to conduct a wedding. But I was a fast learner. I realized that as a preacher, there would be lots of surprises along life's way, and there would be nothing I would be called to do in the service of the Lord that He would not abundantly provide the knowledge and strength to do. And I can tell you that over the years, that has proved to be true.

Howard Townsend was the director of Youth for Christ of Southern California at the time. This wedding was to be something Youth for Christ had never done before, and they wanted to make it an effective Christian extravaganza that would show young people some basic truths and principles of Christian marriage. The wedding was to be a theatrical part of the evening rally and the climax of the program. The speaker's message prior to the wedding would deal with Christian marriage and would strongly emphasize the importance of couples being equally yoked in the bondage of matrimony and not just enter into marriage frivolously.

Carolyn and Tom, along with other couples, had been interviewed and screened for this wedding, and it turned out that God had impressed the committee to select this young, Christian couple to be honored on this special occasion. For me, this was one of the most challenging of the more than 800 weddings I have been privileged to perform during my 60 years of ministry. Nothing in my memory has ever exceeded this one. And how did it all turn out for Carolyn and Tom? Well, it has been *57 years* since that awesome event took place, and Tom and Carolyn are still happily married and have raised a beautiful family. I believe with all my heart that the saying is true: "All ends well that begins well."

When I gave my life to serve the Lord, I sincerely wanted to put my whole heart and soul into giving my very all. If I didn't have an invitation to preach somewhere, I would preach on street corners or anywhere else I could get a crowd. I was determined to find or make a way to preach.

34

Across the street from where I attended seminary was Pershing Square Park. It was always filled with hundreds of people. I believed that this would be a great place for a young preacher like me to practice his calling and made up my mind that this would be my practice field. There was hardly a day during the school week that I didn't go to the park and preach a sermon. I always had an audience of anywhere from 20 to 50 people, who would gather around a park bench and listen to my sermon. It was a place were hundreds of all classes of people went to engage in debate, arguments, conversation, or just sit and enjoy the beauty of the flowers and hear the singing of the birds. It was a great place to get a crowd to listen to just about any subject or for a young preacher to tell people about the love of God and see many souls come to the Lord Jesus.

There is no telling how many sermons I preached in the park during my seminary days. One of the most famous times I can recall was when Billy Graham came to Los Angeles in 1949 for his big tent crusade. The second week of his crusade, rumor had gotten out that Billy Graham was going to be speaking in the park on a certain day. I was oblivious to this, but it just so happened that I was there on that day. The crowd seemed awfully large, and I wondered why. I found a park bench, stepped up on it, and called out to the crowd to come over. And brother, they came! I had the largest crowd I had ever preached to in that park on that day…maybe 200 or 300 people. I couldn't believe it.

I can assure you that the size of the crowd put fire in my bones. I took my New Testament and started quoting Scripture and preaching. There was a lot of noise, so I asked that everyone be as quiet as possible so everyone could hear the message. God was incredibly present—and did the power ever fall! I had the rapt attention of that crowd for about 20 minutes, and when I asked for those who would accept Jesus Christ as Lord and Savior to raise their hand and let me pray for them, there were many hands raised. I reemphasized to them the importance of being dead serious about their decision and not just raising their hands without really meaning it. Still, many hands went back up. So I prayed for them and said, "Amen." Suddenly, a mob rushed forward with outstretched hands to shake my hand. I kept hearing the name "Billy." They were saying, "Billy, we want to shake your hand. We have heard about your big tent meeting." I couldn't believe my ears. I quickly said, "I am not Billy Graham. I am Benny Bates, a student preacher from the seminary across the street." Then I quickly made a dash back to the seminary.

It just so happened that one of the windows at the seminary overlooked the park, and that window just happened to be in the classroom where my evangelism professor, Dr. John PreVoll, taught his class. It was a miracle, but Dr. PreVoll happened to look over into the park that day and notice a very large crowd and someone speaking. Later that day, knowing that it was my practice to preach in the park, he asked if I knew what had taken place over in the park with that large crowd. I told him the story.

I thought that was the end of that, but the next Tuesday, Billy Graham showed up at the seminary to speak in chapel. When Billy came to the podium, he looked out over the student body and said, "I am told there is an impersonator attending your seminary." Everyone began looking around, and suddenly I knew that for some reason Dr. PreVoll had told Billy about my great day in the park. Billy then said, "Will that young man please stand up?" After a moment of hesitation and embarrassment, I sheepishly rose to my feet. Billy related the story to everyone about what had taken place. Of course, the student body and faculty burst forth

36

with laughter and applause, and a number of the faculty and student body had fun with this for several days.

During the 1949 tent meetings, preachers were invited to sit on the platform each night when Billy preached. Every night for weeks, I sat less than six feet from his pulpit, and I became well acquainted with him during this time. As I was thinking back on this interesting moment in my life, I wrote to Dr. Graham and refreshed his memory of this 60-year-old story. He quickly responded with a very kind and warm letter, thanking me for reminding him of this memorable incident and expressing his joy at having heard from me. That meant so much to me.

Chapter 6

Road Trip Revival

IT WAS DURING the summer of 1949 that I really began to feel and experience what the life and work of a minister was all about. I recall that I had often talked with Doc Dishner, one of my dear friends and a member of the band of brothers, about how wonderful it would be for us to take off for a month and make a trip across country, stopping at road-side parks, small-town country stores, and any place where we could get a few people together to witness to and minister our hearts out for the Lord. Doc had a 1940 Chevrolet that was in great shape and a Mobil credit card. He said that we would put all of our gas charges on the card and trust God to lead us as to which route to take—"Route 66" or the southern route. We would just put our lives into His hands and see how many people we could witness to— and maybe some church would open its doors to us and let us minister to them.

Before leaving on this long journey, I went to the president of the seminary, shared our plans with him, and requested his prayers and blessings. I asked him if he would

Picture of Dr. Ben and Doc

see if some of my professors would write a short letter of commendation that we could share with pastors whom we might come into contact with along the way. He was willing to help and spoke to several of my professors about the idea. As a result, seven professors wrote nice letters of introduction and commendation, and with that, we began to plan our trip. With the prayer of our band of brothers and the blessing of our church, family, and many friends, we bade farewell to our wives on a Sunday morning and started out on our uncharted 5,000-mile journey.

Our first stop after leaving Los Angeles, our home base, was Williams, Arizona. We got there about 10 o'clock the first evening and checked into a hotel. Doc was an extremely early riser, and the next morning, without waking me up, he slipped out of bed and went for a walk and prayer time. At about 8 o'clock, he came back all excited and told me about a Baptist church he had found with a sign advertising a revival meeting at 10 o'clock that morning. He told me to get up and get dressed, and then we would have breakfast and head down to the meeting.

When we arrived at the church at about 9:30, only the pastor was there. We introduced ourselves as servants of the Lord who were on a faith mission to travel across the nation, giving our testimony, witnessing to as many lost people as would listen, and having street meetings in the small towns we came to. I pointed to the loud speakers mounted on the roof of our 1940 Chevrolet and told the pastor that we used them to play gospel songs and reach people with the gospel. I told the pastor—whose name I have forgotten—that we wanted to take time to hear their evangelist and then be on our way.

It was then that the pastor shared with us that the evangelist's mother had passed away the day before—the first day of the revival—and that he had canceled the meeting and gone back home. I looked at Doc, he looked at me, and then the wheels began to turn in our minds. I recall that I said to the pastor, "My brother, maybe God sent us here this morning for another reason than to visit your revival service. I am a student evangelist from the California Baptist Seminary in Los Angeles, Doc is a lay preacher, and we have credentials from the school. Maybe you would like to go ahead with your meeting and let us be your servants."

The pastor looked at us with the strangest expression on his face and then said, "You boys come on in and let's pray about this idea. Then I'll let you know how I feel." So we went into the preacher's study and got down on our knees. The pastor prayed first, and then Doc began praying. Doc had a soft heart, and sometimes he would break down and weep as he prayed. Well, that's what happened this time, and it was genuine. Then I prayed out of the depth of my soul. When we were finished, the pastor got up, looked at us, and said, "Boys, I believe God sent you to finish the job."

Did we ever rejoice and praise the Lord! We told the pastor that we would put on gospel records and cover the city of Williams. We would go up and down every street, playing songs and advertising that the revival meeting at the Baptist church would go on tonight and throughout the week as planned. We would tell the people that two new evangelists had come to carry on the services. From the way we built ourselves up, I imagine that people thought that Billy Graham himself had come to carry on the revival.

The preacher asked us to come to his home, and his family would make room for us. He had a wife, two girls, and a large collie dog. I recall that he said, "We will give you a place to sleep and feed you your meals." Dear God, we had no idea what we were getting into, or we might have slipped away without further notice. When we visited the home, the odor was so strong that we almost lost our breath. The house was terribly unkempt. The big collie was asleep on the couch. Dishes were piled up in the sink. The pastor said, "Come on in boys, and I will show you to your room, where you will be sleeping." He took us to the upstairs bedroom, where the two daughters slept. The bed was unmade, and dirty clothes were strewn everywhere. He said, "Boys, it isn't much, but it's the best we can offer."

Doc and I knew we didn't have money to stay in the hotel for a week, so for lack of a better choice, we took his offer. Oh, what a horrible experience. That bed hadn't been changed in days, and the dog had been sleeping on it with the girls. Thankfully, it was summertime, and we didn't need covers at night, so we took the mattress off the bed every evening and slept on the inner springs. The next morning, we would put the mattress back on the bed and go down for breakfast. We were there six mornings for breakfast, and every single morning we had fried bologna with hard scrambled eggs, coffee, and toast. The menu *never* changed. Doc was a rather finicky eater, and I thought he would lose it many times. Every time we would sit down on the couch or on one of the chairs, we would have to pick dog hair off of our clothes for the next 30 minutes.

We had a morning service at 10 o'clock. Doc would speak at that service, and I would lead the singing. At the evening service, I would preach and Doc would lead the singing. During the afternoon, we would cover the town and all the residential areas, playing Jack Holcomb and other gospel records over the sound system as we drove for miles. Doc would tell the people about Evangelist Benny Bates, the "Arkansas Born Tornado." He made it sound so convincing that if they didn't come to the revival service they would be missing two of the greatest preachers to ever come to Williams. Doc would say over the loudspeaker, "Come early to get a good seat." This would go on for at least two hours each day as we promoted our "never–before-heard-of ministry." And as unbelievable as it may sound, God used two unpolished, unprepared, unheard-of, but available young men more than you could ever imagine.

I still wonder what sermons I preached. How I would like to recall even one of them to this day! Whatever I preached, the people must have either come out of curiosity or pity, because the church was literally packed from wall to wall, from front to back, for every evening service, and there were at least 75 people for the morning services. As I recall, the church seated about 300 people, which made it seem to us like a very large preaching place. The largest crowd I had ever spoken to before was at my first sermon in my church back in California. To step into the pulpit at my first revival meeting and face a packed house was a bit exciting.

Every evening, the pastor would get up, brag on us, tell the people about the mission we were on, and say that every one of them ought to make a generous gift to our faith ministry, for we trusted the Lord to meet our needs. I recall how he would plead as he asked the people to support our faith ministry. He would tell them that we were traveling on a Mobile credit card and that we had less than 25 dollars in our pockets. It was true that we were putting all of our gas charges on the credit card. The price of gas was 15 cents per gallon. You could go into a restaurant and get a complete meal for 50 to 75 cents. They tell me a steak dinner would cost no more than one dollar and 50 cents, but Doc and I lived on hamburgers and hot dogs most of the time. It was true that we probably didn't have 25 dollars between us. We ate lots of crackers and peanut butter and bologna sandwiches. We were truly traveling by faith.

Every night as the offering plates returned, they would be filled with bills. This went on for seven days, Monday through Sunday night. On the Sunday afternoon at the close of the revival, the pastor baptized a great host of converts. That Sunday evening, he made a strong plea for another liberal offering for us. When the plates were returned and placed on the Lord's Supper table before the pulpit, they were filled to overflowing. I recall Doc saying with great thanksgiving in his heart, "Benny, the Lord surely is going to supply our financial needs through this wonderful offering."

After the evening service, we packed up and got ready to start driving to Oklahoma City, where Doc's former pastor, Dr. Paul Roberts, the pastor of a very large church, was at that very time conducting his own tent meeting in the city. As we were getting ready to leave, the pastor came out to the car carrying our love offering in a large paper bag that was rolled down at the top and had a string tied around it. He said, "Boys, there is no way to tell you what your ministry has meant to this church and even this town. Here is your offering. We will never forget you—never!"

I remember getting down on my knees by the car in sincere humility and deep sincerity and thanking God for the opportunity to minister and for the great victories we had seen. I got up and said my thank you to the pastor and those standing around the car, and then Doc and I got in the car and started driving. Doc took the wheel first, and I went fast asleep for about three hours. Finally, he woke me up and said, "Benny, I can't wait to know how much money they gave us. Why don't you spread out that atlas and see if you can count it?" I reached back behind the seat and brought out the bag. When I poured out the contents, I discovered that it wasn't all money! Someone had torn up a newspaper and placed it in the bag. In fact, the offering amount was under 30 dollars!

Doc threw on the breaks and pulled off the highway and said we were going to turn around and get our money. We were both in serious shock, because we had seen full offering plates night after night, and we both knew that our offering had been stolen. I said to Doc, "It wouldn't do any good. We would probably get thrown in jail. And what kind of testimony would that be for two preachers? Besides, we can't prove anything. If he can live with it, then let's leave it up to God to deal with that sorry preacher."

With that, we started driving toward Oklahoma City. But neither of us closed our eyes to sleep that night. We were thinking about the greatest ministry experience of our life and how our offering had been stolen by the pastor of the church where God had used our inexperienced lives in such a dynamic way.

Chapter 7

Baptism Back Home

Arriving the next day in Oklahoma City, we went to the home of Dr. Paul Roberts. We arrived there in the early afternoon and after a visit, some good home cooking, and sharing about our experience in Williams, Arizona, Dr. Roberts and his family showed us to a bedroom, where we got a couple of hours of sleep. Later on, we went to the great tent revival where Dr. Roberts was preaching and where we were able to share our testimony. What a thrill it was to speak to about 2,000 people in that big tent.

After our one-night stay with Dr. and Mrs. Roberts, Doc and I drove on to my parents' home near Little Rock. Doc spent the night and then went on his preaching and witnessing mission to South Carolina, where he ministered among his people for two weeks. While Doc was in South Carolina, I was able to see God do some mighty things in my hometown. I was back where I had grown up on the farm with four other brothers. How wonderful it was to be home with family again.

There were so many old friends whom I wanted to see and visit. I inquired about visiting with the pastor of the local Baptist church where our family had belonged and where I became a member in 1940. I learned that the pastor was away on vacation. Some of my lifelong friends soon learned that I was on a preaching and witnessing mission and asked if I would like to preach at an unplanned revival in the community. Of course, I was thrilled, but I told them in all fairness that their pastor needed to be aware of what they were planning and that he should be contacted to see how he felt. One of the deacons got in touch with the pastor, and he was much in favor of the idea and gave his blessing.

Shortly thereafter, 20 to 30 people in the community began to tell their friends that Benny Bates, one of their own boys whom God had called to preach, was home and was willing to preach an unscheduled revival in the auditorium of the community school house. This was a neutral location that seated about 250 people and was more likely to attract people from other churches. Soon, people from all over the community began to receive and pass the word on to their friends. When the meeting opened on Tuesday evening—my second revival meeting—the house was packed. For the next five nights, people came from as far away as 15 miles, which was a far piece in 1950 to go hear a preacher—especially a preacher who was preaching his second revival meeting.

To my great surprise, pick-up trucks came loaded with young people. Some people even came on their tractors, pulling a flatbed trailer loaded with young and old alike from the farm community where I grew up. Every night, the crowds were overflowing; some even drove from Little Rock, which was 18 miles away. Many of my former schoolmates came to hear me preach for the first time. One night, most of the basketball team that I had played with in high school attended. Many of my old school buddies and former teachers and friends also came.

There were a great number of people converted to salvation, both young and old alike. After the service each evening, anywhere from 5 to 15 people would line up across the front of the auditorium to be greeted as their loved ones and friends came by to rejoice with them for the decision they had made. When the meeting came to an end, I asked the church to vote to receive those desiring membership by transfer of letter and for baptism into the Toltec Baptist Church, where I was once a member.

The baptism was scheduled to take place in the Arkansas River near Scott, Arkansas, about 10 miles from the community where we had the meeting. Among the converts were two of my brothers, plus a host of loved ones, former schoolmates, and lifetime friends. Having never baptized anyone, I called on Brother W. C. Halsell, a beloved preacher I had known from the time I was a small boy and one of the dearest and godliest men I ever knew, to teach me how to baptize. I will never forget his instruction: "Now, Benny, when you baptize the men, you make sure to ask them to wrap their pocketbook in plastic, and baptize them with their pocketbooks. You tell them that now they have taken the Lord as Savior, they are to faithfully give one-tenth of their income to the work of the Lord."

I remember following Brother Halsell's explicit instructions. O, what a glorious sight it was to see that long line of new converts reaching from the bank's edge of the river and extending far out into the water. I will never forget that awesome event and scene. I can close my eyes now, almost 60 years later, and see that never-to-be-forgotten scene. It was an old-fashioned, country baptizing that some of you have probably never seen the likes of. It was a hallelujah time on the bank of the Arkansas River.

Chapter 8

The Fundraiser

THESE TWO GLORIOUS weeks of being with the people I had grown up with, unexpectedly ministering and sharing the good news of the Word of God, seeing large numbers of converts come to the Lord, and being able to baptize my first converts, was one of the truly high points of my early ministry. When these two weeks were over, my dear friend Doc came back for me, and after a last meal prepared by my sweet mother that was fit for royalty and a final night with my family, we were on our way back to California.

Doc and I made many stops on our way back. Whenever we saw a carload of people stranded or stopped alongside the road, we would stop to witness to them. We even saw some accept Jesus. Whenever we saw a roadside park where there were people resting, we would stop and play a gospel song over the loudspeaker and witness to them. We passed out thousands of gospel tracts throughout the more than 5,000 miles we traveled.

It was terribly hot as we traveled across the desert, and there was no air conditioning in automobiles in those days. As we approached one small Arizona town, in which the temperature was well over 100 degrees, the timing gear chain went out on Doc's car, and we were stranded for a day and a half. The little motel we spent the night in was not air-conditioned, and there was not even a circulating fan. What a miserable night. However, that was the only car trouble we experienced during the entire trip. There is no way I can possibly relate how God poured out His blessings on us! The glory of those wonderful days is still vividly etched in my memory. That experience taught me that if God could use two young and inexperienced men as He used us on that 5,000-mile journey, He could use anyone.

Arriving back home in California, Doc and I were so thrilled to have completed such a long journey with no major incidents that we got down on our knees, kissed the earth, and praised God that He had blessed us so greatly and brought us back safely. We had so many stories to share with our band of brothers, the people at church, and our families. When another semester at seminary began shortly after I returned home, I was able to share with my professors and classmates many of the wonderful stories of what we had experienced on our 5,000-mile trip for Jesus.

Shortly after starting back to class, I was called to my first student pastorate at the Montebello Baptist Church. Bettie and I saw many wonderful things happen there, and the experience was helpful, but it was only a short ministry that lasted about six months. I was getting so many invitations for weekend engagements and revivals in the area that I felt it was the will of the Lord for me to ask the church to call one of my school buddies to be the pastor. This worked out well. The church grew, and my seminary friend had a great ministry for many months.

Of course, all of these engagements brought some problems with them that I had to face. I was spending so much time preaching that there was not enough time for my studies. Going back to school in my mid-twenties, carrying a full load of subjects, and preaching almost constantly wasn't going to be easy. For me to carry on the scale of ministry I was committing myself to as a young preacher and maintain passing grades in school, I needed a different plan. So I persuaded some of my upper-class student friends to tutor me in some of the more difficult subjects so that I could do all the extra work I was doing and still make passing grades. I found two or three people who were happy to get the few extra bucks, and I was thrilled to have the help.

I shall never forget one incident that occurred during this time. One of my professors often came to hear me preach when I was speaking at a revival or a church in the area. Of course, this was always a thrill for me, as I would see him out in the audience taking notes. This inspired me and made me feel good—until I found out he was writing down all of my misuses of words and bad grammar. One day, he called me into his office and talked with me for about an hour, strongly urging me to seek some special help with my grammar. When I left his office, I went straight to the college English professor and told her that I needed help. Thank the Lord, I got help from the English department at the college as well as from several upper-class English students who spent many hours with me. I have never ceased to thank God for their help. I know, even now I get a little careless, but just be glad you didn't know me back then.

Months passed, and my seminary days were coming to a close. One of the seminary officials approached me and asked me to speak in different churches in the area to enlist Sunday School departments, classes, and even congregations in adopting some of the students for the purpose of helping with their tuition. Those who were married were especially having a difficult time staying in school. This turned out to be a tremendous idea, because many churches responded to the need. It became the very lifeline that made it possible for many married students to remain in school. I was blessed in that I had the G.I. Bill, a pension from the Navy, and the salary of my wife, who got her PHT ("Putting Husband Through") degree, to give me support.

After several weeks, the program was working so well that I was asked to help raise special funds to purchase a million-dollar campus in Covina, California, so the school could move out of the downtown Los Angeles area and reach more students. My first assignment was to call on Mr. Walter Knott, the founder of Knott's Berry Farm, located in Buena Park, California. Founded in 1928, this nationally known theme park became best known for its fried chicken dinners and boysenberry pie desserts. The purpose of my visit was to seek a financial donation from Mr. Knott to help our seminary purchase the new campus.

This was another experience that made me tremble. Just imagine a young 30-year-old walking into this great man's office and brazenly asking him for a large gift to help a small seminary that he maybe had never even heard of. When I met with Mr. Knott, I shared with him the story of our seminary and showed him pictures of the school's ministry and student body. I told him how God had increased the student body to the point in which we were now out of space and had to relocate. Mr. Knott had a number of questions, which I evidently answered to his satisfaction. After our visit was over, he called his secretary into his office and asked her to write a check to the California Baptist Seminary to be used toward the purchase of their new campus at Covina. The check was sizeable, and my excitement was rising by the moment—I wanted to hurry back to the school and break the good news.

I put the check into my pocket and warmly shook hands with Mr. Knott, thanking him for his great generosity, and then I humbly dismissed myself. When I arrived back at the seminary, I couldn't wait to flash this gift before the president. All the way back, the old flesh nature was raising its ugly head, and I was saying to myself, *Man, they are going to be so proud of you. They will probably have you up before the student body and heap compliments on you. You might even be given an honorary doctor's degree some day for this large gift that you were able to bring to the school.* Satan was having his field day for a few moments in my thoughts.

When I went to deliver the check to Mr. Diltz Cole, the public relations director, I was just beaming with joy. He received me warmly, with hearty handshakes and hugs, gratefully thanked me, and then said, "We knew you could do it; now go and keep on going." Well, I never was able to top that wonderful miracle, but in due time, the seminary was able to purchase the land, and the school moved to the beautiful location nestled in the rolling hills of Covina.

Chapter 9

The Joys and Challenges of Evangelism

AFTER SEMINARY, I chose to enter the field of full-time evangelism. This would be a ministry in which I would be totally depending on the Lord for my livelihood. However, before I could really go out on my own, Youth for Christ International invited me to come on board as one of their international evangelists. This led to my traveling extensively across California and Oregon to speak at Youth for Christ citywide rallies. I couldn't believe that I was on the same circuit with men like Dr. Bob Cook, Tory Johnson, Dr. Mervin Rozell, Ted and Gloria Roe, Billy Graham, and other greats. It was a great and humbling experience and such a thrill to speak at Youth for Christ rallies that were filled to capacity with teenagers, young people, and adults. It seemed so easy to challenge and reach the youth of that era. If only we could see those wonderful days return.

My ministry with the International Youth for Christ organization led to many wonderful experiences. The Saturday night rallies were a sight to behold. Even far more exciting was to be a part of the rallies. It was thrilling to see

30 to 40 youth and adults responding at invitation time to accept Jesus Christ as their Lord and Savior. Many of the high school Bible clubs across the nation were sponsored by Youth for Christ, and these led many thousands of people to Jesus Christ as Savior.

Working with Youth for Christ demanded a rigorous schedule and meant that I was constantly away from home. I began to ask the Lord to open up a ministry where I could have more time with my wife and new son. It wasn't long until my prayer was answered, and the Lord opened the door to my first major pastorate: the First Southern Baptist Church of Baldwin Park, California. In those days, Baldwin Park was a rather small town. The church offered a great challenge, and I dove in with both feet—actually, with more enthusiasm and brawn than knowledge. I started out full speed to win the whole city for Christ.

Things happened quickly. We embarked on a massive campaign to visit every home in the area. Participation was overwhelming, and people started responding. Soon, the church was so packed that we had to go to two services and provide new educational space to take care of the Sunday School and Training Union attendance. We baptized people at almost every service. On our first Easter at Baldwin Park, we held our main service out on the front lawn, in the open air. More than 500 people attended. Reporters from the local newspaper came and took pictures, and a huge, front-page story about the service and growth of the church was published.

At that time, I began a radio ministry called "The Voice of Youth." The program was aired over ABC in the California area. The message was designed to reach the younger generation, yet still be appealing to adults. I had a great cast of people who worked with me on the 30-minute broadcast that aired on Sunday afternoon following Billy Graham's "Hour of

Decision." Ted and Gloria Roe, one of the most noted musical teams in the Southern California area, were in charge of the musical segment of the program. Norman Nelson, one of the great lyric tenors of the day, was my soloist, and we had one of the finest ladies' trios in all of California.

"The Voice of Youth" had many listeners and was professional in every way...well, maybe except for the preaching! We got many letters and compliments, but, as in almost everything, there was a weakness. The broadcast was at the mercy of freewill offerings given by the listening audience, and within less than a year, we had to shut it down. It was interesting to have people come up to me when I was conducting a revival meeting or preaching somewhere in the state and say to me that they had listened to the broadcast and missed it being on the air.

The ministry at Baldwin Park was exciting and fruitful. It was the first real pastorate in which I had the opportunity to organize and grow a well-rounded ministry. It was the place where I really got my practical experience as a pastor. It was a proving ground, where I was able to experiment with growth ideas and learn what God could and could not use. It was a place where I could discover what would stimulate Christians to serve and be faithful in the service of the Lord.

After serving in the Baldwin Park First Southern Baptist Church, I was called to be pastor of the First Southern Baptist Church of Pasadena, California, home to the Tournament of Roses. While I was serving in this church, I was invited to speak for a group of motion picture actors who met regularly for inspiration, prayer, and fellowship in the home of Dale and Roy Rogers. It was an experience I shall never forget. Dale and Roy had been my idols during my teen years, and never in a lifetime did I expect to meet them in person. I found them to be simply wonderful and down-to-earth people as I fellowshipped with them that night.

The First Southern Baptist Church, Pasadena, CA

I met so many of Hollywood's finest Christian stars that evening. Among the warm and friendly new friends I made, I met a young actor and his wife, Gregory and Barbara Walcott, who stood out in the crowd like two glittering diamonds. Greg and Barbara became two of our closest friends and were in our home on many occasions. Several times, Greg gave his incredible testimony to our congregation at the First Southern Baptist Church of Pasadena. Greg even made a special appearance at one of my crusades in Salinas, California. It was immediately after his big hit movie *Texas Lady*, in which was the leading male star with Claudette Colbert. Someone arranged to have Greg ride down Main Street on a beautiful horse, decked out in full Western regalia. This was a spectacular sight, and his appearance was a great contribution to the crusade.

I remember so many special times when the four of us were together. Greg and Barbara loved Bettie's special enchiladas and the other Mexican food she would prepare, and they would drive over to Pasadena to kick back with

Left to right: Barbara Walcott, Greg Walcott, Roy Rogers, and Dale Evans

us. What a time of fellowship we would have. Once, we thought it would be fun for the four of us to get together and stroll down Hollywood Boulevard to window shop and watch the people. On our stroll, we went into an ice cream parlor and had such fun talking and laughing. I'm sure others around us thought we were four crazy people, the way we were carrying on.

We have kept up our friendship with Greg and Barbara through the years, and even today we stay in touch over the Internet. I could not make a better recommendation than to ask you to add *Hollywood Adventures: The Gregory Walcott Story* to your reading list. For 40 years, Greg has remained one of the best character actors in the business. He has appeared in more than 50 movies and 300 television shows and has worked with scores of talented performers throughout his illustrious career. Greg and Barbara are born-again believers.

One of Greg's greatest Christian contributions was the *Bill Wallace of China* story, which he starred in and produced in 1967. The movie told the true story of a Tennessee Christian missionary doctor who died in a Chinese prison in 1949. The University of Tennessee hosted the world premier, and funds from the premier benefit were used to establish the Bill Wallace Memorial Library section at the University. Also in 1967, Georgetown University of Lexington, Kentucky, awarded Greg an honorary Doctor of Law degree, recognizing his film career and civic activities.

We were at the First Southern Baptist Church of Pasadena just two short years before the Lord permitted me to return to full-time, local church evangelism. I was recognized by the California Baptist State Convention and approved as a convention evangelist. I had always known that evangelism was my first love. I loved preaching as a pastor, but there was always that strong pull on my heart to start a new meeting and meet new friends and preach to new crowds and watch the Holy Spirit work in the saving of lost souls and see the lives of Christians stirred to new life and new commitment. I know that I am privileged to have evangelized during the "glory days" of evangelism in the fifties and sixties. At almost every church where one would preach a revival, you could expect capacity crowds, if the church had done its homework. The fifties were really the most fruitful years for seeing maximum attendance at these revivals and witnessing people being converted and uniting with churches.

The excitement of seeing the responses night after night and having so many non-church people in the services was so different from modern-day evangelism. On the other hand, the constant grind of travelling and spending much time away from home took its toll. After month after month of this lifestyle, I again began asking the Lord to open up a ministry that would give me more time with my family. At this time, our first child, Carey, was very young, and I missed being with him when I was away from home. Telephoning long distance was rather expensive in those days, and we could not afford for me to call home every night. Oh, if only cell phones had been invented and the calling rates had been as they are today! It is hard for the younger generation to realize that in the fifties and sixties it was an altogether different day. Some of the love offerings we evangelists received were often on the short end, and we had to be careful with our funds.

I once preached a revival in a rather large church, with a congregation of more than 800 people. We had witnessed a great response of people making decisions, and on the final Friday and Saturday evenings and in the Sunday morning service, the pastor received the love offering. He was passionate in his request for the people to give. I was to leave following the morning service to begin another meeting in different city that evening. But then the pastor said to me, "I want you to go back there where they are counting the three offerings and make sure you get all of your money." I was stunned. I said, "Pastor, I can't do that. Surely they will give me what the people gave." The pastor said, "Don't be so sure of that. I don't trust some of them."

At his insistence, I went back to where they were counting the love offering. There was a thin partition that separated me from where they were. I could hear the conversation, and one of the counters said, "You know, this seems to be a very large amount in this envelope to give to the evangelist. Let us give him this amount." The pastor had slipped into the room by this time and heard the comment. He was irate. He walked into the counting room and said, "Brethren, I heard the remark that it seemed too much to give the evangelist so large an offering and that we should give him this amount. Brethren, I have told the people that the offering they were giving was for the evangelist, whose livelihood depends on what he receives from freewill offerings. I will take the total offering and see that every cent goes to our faithful evangelist."

All the time I served in evangelism, I never put an amount or stipulation on my freewill offerings. I simply trusted God to supply my needs. On the other hand, I never thought that any church would withhold funds that were especially designated to my love offering.

Although I found the field of mass evangelism to be fruitful and exciting, I also found it to be a difficult ministry in some ways. About 70 percent of the churches would follow suggested preparation plans and work diligently to have everything ready so that a great outpouring of God's Spirit would occur when the evangelist arrived. Oh, the blessedness of victories and results that came from those churches that faithfully prepared and got their congregation ready. But oh, what a drag the services would be when there was little or no preparation!

After the birth of our son in 1950, it became harder for me to stay away from home for an extended length of time. I recall that when our son was about 15 months old and I came home from a two-week crusade, he would run to his mother, hide behind her, and refuse to come to me or let me pick him up for a while. I found the loneliness of being away from my family for two or three weeks to be unbearable. Sometimes, when the evening service at a revival was over, I would go to my room in the home I had been assigned, and the walls would seem to close in on me with loneliness for my family and friends back home.

In those days, churches didn't often put the evangelist in a hotel or motel. Generally, you would be asked to stay in a private home, which was not always the most desired way to go. I could tell many stories about that arrangement. All too often the host and hostess felt they had to entertain the evangelist, and when you came home after the service, they would want to visit and fellowship. I would be tired and wanted nothing more than to call it a day. Many were the times I would close out a meeting and drive 100 to 200 miles to get home and spend some quality time with my wife and son for a few days before leaving for another meeting or series of meetings to do battle with the devil again.

When I was away from home, my day normally consisted of having breakfast with the family I was staying with (on their time schedule). My usual custom was to spend a couple of hours studying for the morning worship service at 10 o'clock. It was customary to have a morning service back in the fifties and sixties, and after the service I would be expected to go to some home and have a big lunch (or have lunch at the church). After lunch, I would normally go back to my room and prepare for the evening message until about 3 o'clock. The pastor or some laymen and I would then visit until 5 o'clock, witnessing to people and inviting them to the revival. Generally, some family would prepare a big supper for the evangelist and singer every evening at 5:30. After the meal and a time of visiting with the family, it would be time to rush to the church for a 7 o'clock pre-revival prayer service.

The service always began at 7:30. Ninety percent of the time, the church would be filled, and without exception, you could count on having a number of unsaved persons present to hear God's Word. There was never any sense of a rush or an urgency to end the service by a certain time. Typically, the services ended by 9 o'clock, or even 9:30, if the Holy Spirit was doing something very special. Even then, folks would linger, visit, love, and enjoy one another. We hardly ever had a service in which people were not being saved and joining the church.

I can hardly describe the memory of some of those days. How I pray for the day when the church returns to evangelistic meetings like we had in those glorious times. But it is my humble opinion that we will never experience times like that with the little preparation that is made in the average meeting of today. It is impossible to see a mighty working of the Holy Spirit accomplished in a three-day "mini revival" that takes place in most church revivals of today.

We had prayed for the Lord to bless us with a baby girl. God heard and answered that prayer on October 13, 1953, when He sent us a precious daughter, Dodie, to grace our lives. What a blessing our precious children have been! We committed them to the Lord as infants, and now for many years they have been in the ministry of our Savior.

Our Grandchildren (one not present)

My son, Carey, and his wife, Lynne, became missionaries to Portugal and spent 10 years harvesting for the Lord. When they left America, they took two of our four grandchildren far away from us. While they were serving in Portugal, it was our great fortune to be able to visit them on four occasions. Once, I had the great thrill of taking our daughter, Dodie, with me, and the three of us ministered in many areas. I would get to preach, and they provided the entertainment through music and song. While my son was in Portugal, a third grandchild was born. Years have passed, and now all three have graduated from college and are out on their own. Hudson, the youngest, just signed a contract to play professional volleyball in Puerto Rico. The other two have great jobs and are doing well.

Our precious daughter, Dodie, and her husband, Walter, have three children: Beth Ann, Walter Jr., and Bettie Dianne. All three of their children are married and doing well. Beth is working with a church and at State Farm in Phoenix,

Arizona. Bettie is employed with State Farm in Winter Haven, Florida, and Walter Jr. is a minister of youth for a church in Lynchburg, Virginia. I don't have to tell you that our six grandchildren fill our hearts with great joy. We rejoice and thank God for favoring us with far more than we could ask as parents and grandparents. What is especially so wonderful is that they all know the Lord Jesus Christ as their personal Savior. Bettie and I are proud of the heritage that God has given us.

Chapter 10

A New Assignment

BETTIE AND I didn't know it, but the Lord was getting ready to move us from California after many glorious years spent there in His service. However, before the move, I felt the Lord had one more city-wide tent crusade He wanted me to preach. This last California evangelistic crusade came about through a visit I made to Bill Zachary, one of my wonderful friends who was a commercial real estate broker.

Bill was one of the greatest soul winners I have ever known. His greatest love was to pick up hitchhikers and tell them about Jesus. Driving on a cross-country trip one time, Bill saw two dirty-looking young men on the side of the road, pulled over, and told them to get in. When they got comfortable, Bill began telling them about Jesus. This went on for about 45 minutes. They came to a roadside restaurant, and Bill pulled in and said, "Boys, you look like you could eat a big steak. Come on in, and let's have lunch." They ate and then started traveling again.

About 50 miles down the road, Bill had brought both of them to confess Jesus Christ as their Lord and Savior. When the two men arrived at their destination, one of them reached in his boot, pulled out a pistol, and said to Bill, "When you picked us up, we had plans to kill you and take your new Lincoln. But you and God changed our mind." Bill handed them a 50-dollar bill, prayed with them, and drove away.

As Bill and I visited that day, I told him of my burden to conduct a large seven-cities tent crusade in the San Gabriel valley. Bill was excited. As we talked, I explained that such a crusade would cost a great deal of money and that I needed someone who could put up the finances to get the crusade through a planning stage. I was surprised when Bill quickly said, "I will put up the money. Whatever it takes to fund the crusade." Bill's next question was, "What next?" I told him that we would need to contact the ministers in the San Gabriel valley to enlist their support and that we would need a crusade committee of pastors and laymen to approve such a crusade and commit to sponsor it with their churches.

During the next 12 weeks, things began to move. When there was a need for funds to be disbursed up front, Bill would provide the money. We elected a treasurer, who kept careful records of all money spent. Scores of pre-campaign meetings were held. The Reverend Cummins (Sam) Lovett, a beloved friend and seminary mate who was noted for his personal soul-winning skills, was put in charge of organizing a team of personal workers to handle those who would be making decisions for Christ and to channel prospects to pastors of various churches. We held many training sessions to make certain that everything was covered and in order. Finally, we erected a large tent in a central location a week before the start of the crusade and enlisted one of the finest musical teams in California to be in charge of all the music.

The crusade kicked off on a Saturday evening with a capacity crowd. Services were held nightly at 7:30 and at 3 o'clock each Sunday afternoon for three weeks. A great number of souls were saved, and many came forward to make other decisions. It was a thrilling three weeks. The offering for the first two weeks covered all the expenses of the crusade. Out of this one great meeting, scores of people came to Christ, including one group of converts who, along with a local Baptist minister, started a Baptist church that later grew into a large congregation in West Covina.

Dr. Ben Preaching at a Tent Crusade

Following this crusade, some great changes took place in my life and ministry. In 1956, I traveled from Los Angeles to Little Rock, Arkansas, to preach at a revival crusade held at the West Side Baptist Church, a church at which I had previously preached two crusades in the past. I stopped off in Tulsa, Oklahoma, to visit with Dr. Ted and Gloria Roe and meet new friends. While I was there, Dr. Roe invited me to stay over and preach at Sheridan Road Baptist Church's Wednesday evening service before going on to Little Rock. I agreed, but I didn't know at the time that he had notified two pulpit committees to come hear me.

After the service, six nicely dressed individuals quickly made their way to me and introduced themselves as the pulpit committee from the First Baptist Church of Tahlequah, Oklahoma. I had never heard of the place—I could hardly pronounce it and surely couldn't spell it—but they wanted to take me out for a steak dinner and talk with me. We had a long meeting at a nice steak house until about 11 o'clock, and I agreed to drop by and preach for them *if* I could persuade the Little Rock pastor to let me start the meeting on Monday evening. I called the church in Little Rock and spoke with the pastor and asked him if he could make it right with the church to let me begin on Monday evening instead of Sunday. Of course, he was willing, and so I preached for the church in Tahlequah, Oklahoma, a college town in Northeaster, Oklahoma, and the capitol of the Cherokee nation.

I arrived at the church with mixed emotions, for I had never conceived of becoming a pastor...let alone a pastor in *Oklahoma*. The church had done an incredible job of spreading the word that a new prospective pastor would be preaching and had urged the people to fill the house. I preached, and during the first and only meeting with that congregation, I felt impressed that a tremendous evangelistic opportunity waited for me in this college town of some 6,000 students. After I preached, some of the members asked me to step into the office that joined the auditorium, where I could pretty well hear everything they were saying.

Actually, I have to confess that I stood with my ear to the door for some of the time and listened. Aren't I terrible? In about 30 minutes, they invited me back and asked if I would permit them to cast a vote of their persuasion to call or not call me as their pastor.

Although they knew very little about me and had only heard me preach one sermon, about 300 members were asked to vote to call me as pastor of their church. It was contrary to all procedure, and it is likely that the incident set a precedent in calling a pastor. The vote was called for in my presence, which was also most unusual, and when the chairman of the committee asked that all who wished to extend a call to me to become their pastor vote, *not one person* voted against me. The chairman of the search committee turned to me and said, "Preacher, we want you to move to Oklahoma! Hopefully, you will seriously pray

First Baptist Church of Tahlequah, Oklahoma (1956)

about our need for a pastor and give us your answer as soon as possible."

Later, I called Bettie and said, "Are you ready for the shock of your life?" She said, "Benny, you are not in any kind of trouble, are you? Have you had an accident? Are you all right?" I said, "Honey, you had better start packing to move to Oklahoma, because I have just been called to be the pastor of the First Baptist Church of Tahlequah." Her first words were, "Where on earth is Tahlequah? Have you lost your mind? You mean we are going to have to move?" I figured that 1,500 miles might be just a little far to commute on weekends and Wednesdays, so I said, "Yep, if I say yes to these people, we are going to have to move." I then told her that the beautiful part was that we would be only about three hours from our parents in Arkansas. Well, that changed the whole picture, and she said, "In that case, I'll start packing."

After preaching at the revival in Little Rock and returning home to California, I began to feel strongly that the church in Tahlequah had made what they believed to be a *right* decision. If these 300 people, who had never met me before and had heard me preach only that one sermon, wanted me to be their pastor, I surely ought to consider it. The church, of course, said they would pay all of our moving costs, but we encountered a problem with selling our home. Bettie and I both agreed that if God were in our decision, He would take care of that matter with no problem. And guess what? He did.

I was out hammering a post in the front lawn, on which I was going to nail a handmade "for sale" sign, when a couple drove by, suddenly stopped, and asked, "Is your home for sale? If so, when may we see it?" I dropped the hammer and said, "You may see it right now if you like." The couple pulled into the drive, and I yelled to Bettie that we had people who wanted to see the house. She was beside herself and said, "Are you out of your mind? It isn't ready to show!"

Well, I won that one, and they walked in and through the house and out into the backyard. Then the man said, "How much are you asking?" I told him the figure. He looked at his wife, and they spoke for a few moments. Then he looked back at me and said, "You've got a sale. We will take it. When can we move in?" When Bettie and I picked ourselves off the ground, I said that we could be out in 15 days. From that moment, we knew that God had given us the green light to move to Oklahoma. I called the church and told them I would accept the position.

The next three and a half years were glorious. Tahlequah was one of the most serene places that one could ever hope to live. We were surrounded by lakes and the beautiful Boston Mountains. The people at the First Baptist Church of Tahlequah were the most caring and loving people I had ever pastored. More than 400 souls were added to the church, and new missions were begun among the Cherokee people in the county.

As I mentioned, Tahlequah is the capitol of the Cherokee nation, and many Indians made up the membership of our church. Some of Bettie's and my closest friends were of the Cherokee lineage. In fact, it is *my* lineage. One of my deacons, after finding out that I was of Cherokee decent, urged me to let him come to my office and teach me the mother tongue. It is such a beautiful language. I always felt that I was too busy to learn it, and I will always regret not doing so.

Because Tahlequah was a college town, we had unbelievable opportunities to minister to the student body through the Baptist Student Union. We were able to reach and baptize a large number of students and involve them in our youth ministry program. It was at Tahlequah that the Lord sent into my life one of the greatest and most loyal servants of God I have ever worked with. We needed ministerial help with a sudden influx of membership, and God sent us Mr. Charles W. Hill and his wife, Judy, to serve with me as minister of education, youth, and music.

What a dynamic team they made. Judy was the greatest children's worker to be found in the entire convention, while Charles was a master at organizing our education ministry and was great with the youth. The Sunday School program began to grow beyond all expectations. In those days we had "Training Union," and it exploded in attendance, which caused the Sunday evening service to be packed. (Training Union was the southern Baptist program in those days that was similar to the "Sunday School" organization that was a one hour event just prior to the evening service.) First Baptist became filled with college young people. In every service, it was common to see numbers of new converts and others coming into the membership by transfer of letter. Charles was actually my first associate minister, and I loved him as my own brother.

One of the evangelistic highlights of our ministry in Tahlequah was when the Lord led us to erect a huge tent, set it up on one of the most strategic locations in the city, and conduct a three-week evangelistic crusade. We engaged the very best song evangelist. John Jolly and his wife, Shirley, were chosen to provide the music. We enlisted great gospel trios and quartets to provide special music each night. I was privileged to be the evangelist. We blanketed the area with posters and advertisements and had radio announcements breaking throughout the day and evening. The newspaper liberally publicized the meeting by sending a photographer to take pictures of the services and a reporter to write and publish articles daily. The response was greater than anyone could have ever thought. God gave many precious souls and additions by transfer of letter to the church. Many other churches participated and reaped many new members into their churches as well.

The board of regents of the college appointed me to be the official chaplain for the Northeastern College football team. That year, they won the national collegiate championship for small colleges. What an honor and great ministry it was to be the spiritual leader for that great football team and their coaches.

The other surprising honor came from the Southern California Seminary, located in the San Diego area, which notified me that I had been chosen to receive the honorary Doctor of Divinity degree and asked me to preach the commencement address for the graduating class of 1958. That was an honor I shall never forget. Upon my return to my church in Tahlequah, the church held a great surprise dinner and congratulations gathering for me. When some of the members asked me what this all meant, I recall telling them that it was like the curl in a pig's tail—a little more style, but no more pig!

Chapter 11

Triumph and Tragedy

FROM OKLAHOMA, GOD called me to pastor the First Baptist Church of Jacksonville, Arkansas, a town of about 15,000 people. Jacksonville is actually the bedroom city of Little Rock and is the home of The Little Rock Air Force base. Both Bettie's parents and my parents lived within 30 minutes to an hour from the church. We had missed living closer to them for a very long time.

The church had been going through a great deal of transition. The two preceding pastors had only stayed a short time before returning to their former pastorates. One had stayed four weeks before returning to his former church, while the other had stayed six weeks. In view of this, I was apprehensive when I first visited the church to preach. I had many questions that needed to be answered before I could show much interest in the position. I had been recommended by seven pastors in the Little Rock area, two of which had more than 3,000 members in their churches. I inquired of them and asked why the two preceding pastors had never unpacked before returning to their former pastorates. I learned that both men had seriously felt they had made terrible mistakes in leaving their former churches and had returned to those respective churches at the constant insistence of their people.

My first visit with the committee and the deacons of the church wiped out any apprehension I had about being called as its pastor. I saw the most promising vision of evangelistic opportunity that I had ever faced in my ministry, because the Little Rock Air Base was located there. The night I preached my trial sermon, the lower auditorium was packed. I strongly felt that this was God's will for me.

After waiting some three weeks to give my answer, I called the committee and told them that I felt the challenge was appealing and that if the church sensed the Lord's leading to issue a call, Bettie and I would come. The church voted, and only one elderly man stood and said, "I think we need an older and more seasoned pastor, and for that reason I vote no." The church called me, and I accepted the position. (Later, that man, my only opposition, became my greatest friend and supporter, and he remained so until the day he went home to be with the Lord.)

Soon, God literally began to open the windows of heaven and pour out blessings and give victories the like of which had never been seen in the history of the First Baptist Church. Within a few short months, we had to add a second Sunday morning service, because we could not accommodate the growing crowds. At this point, I realized we needed help, and my heart turned to Charles Hill, my former Oklahoma associate. Thank God, Charles and Judy agreed to come, and the people at First Baptist fell in love with them at first meeting. Charles came aboard and took charge of our education program, youth ministry, and choir program. Soon, things really began to roll. Our Sunday School increased in attendance to the point that we were out of space and had to go to two Sunday Schools.

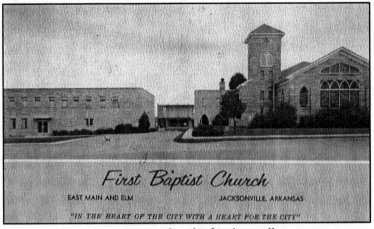

First Baptist Church of Jacksonville

The first year, we baptized people at every Sunday evening service and at many Wednesday evening services. The second year, we had to add a *third* Sunday morning service in order to accommodate the growth, and we began renovations on the auditorium and built a new education building. We started a missions program, and for more than four years we were the leading church in Arkansas in winning and baptizing new converts. More than 1,200 people were received into the church by baptism and by transfer of letter during the four and a half years Bettie and I were there. Our Sunday school attendance surpassed 1,000 on several occasions, and God blessed the work.

One Saturday evening, September 19, 1964, at about 7 o'clock in the evening, I was having dinner with my family when I received a call that stunned me to the depths of my soul. The Jacksonville Chief of Police was on the line, and he abruptly said, "Dr. Bates, you must come quickly to the Beck home. Gerald Beck has just murdered his wife, Rita Beck, and taken his own life." I had dealt with almost every sort of emergency before, but I had never been confronted with the murder and suicide of the members of my church.

Arriving at the scene, the police allowed me to enter the crime scene, where I found *six precious children,* ranging from 16 months to 13 years of age, still in the home. They had witnessed the horrible tragedy of their father killing their mother and then turning the gun on himself. The couple had been divorced for about two months. I did not know Gerald, but I did know Rita. She was a native of England and was a gentle and kind person.

The couple's long martial troubles had made for a turbulent life for Rita and her six children. She had been saving two dollars per week from her salary at the local newspaper to take her children back to England. I had last seen her on the morning of the 16th of September at the local market, where she had confided that she feared for her life because Gerald had threatened to kill her if she tried to take the children away. I knew of their troubles, but I certainly did not dream that it had reached this magnitude. I counseled Rita for a time at the market and told her to call me when it was convenient for us to talk more. I prayed with her, not realizing that this was the last time I would see her alive.

Immediately following the tragic event, I was appointed temporary guardian of the six children and was given instructions to begin obtaining the necessary passports to take the children to Norwich, England, where they would be put under the care of Mr. and Mrs. L. H. Betts, the children's maternal grandparents. As news of the tragic event swept across the state and even across the nation, a fund was established at a local bank, and money began to pour in from almost every county in the state, and even from other states. Thousands of dollars were collected for the purpose of getting the children back to England and establishing them in their new home with their grandparents. But this was not at all easy, because there were a number of complications.

The relatives of the deceased father, after hearing that there would be considerable monetary benefits for the six children from state and federal government agencies, filed a court order to prevent the children from being taken to England. This created a situation that placed a great deal of pressure on the children, most of whom wanted to stay together and go live with their grandparents. We feared the opposition would file a restraining order to prevent us from taking the children as they sought a court order to keep the children in Arkansas with relatives of the deceased father.

However, the Lord worked mightily on behalf of the children. Before the court could serve me a subpoena or any further legal action could be taken to delay the departure, Orval Faubus, the governor of Arkansas, ordered the general in charge of the National Guard to secretly take Mrs. Bates, the six children, and me to an undisclosed motel in Little Rock. The next morning, the general and a fleet of cars arrived to take us to the plane that was waiting for us at the end of one of the runways at the Little Rock National Airport. We quickly boarded and took off for Atlanta, Georgia, where we would board a flight to London.

My wife, Bettie, who had fallen in love with the children, accompanied us to Atlanta but did not make the journey to England. I look back on that event and wonder how I ever managed with six children. Had it not been for the fact that the pilot and flight attendants had been apprised of the tragedy, it would have been impossible. Thankfully, the flight was not full, and once we were airborne, each of the children had his or her own private attendant. The six children had never before received the royal treatment they were given on this long flight over the ocean. They were given all they desired in the way of food and attention. Fact of the matter is, I don't think I have ever been treated so royally or dined so elegantly in all my life.

The pilot got on the speaker and explained that there was a special group aboard. He briefly explained a bit about the situation and asked if the people sitting in a certain section of the aircraft would mind moving to other seats—even to first class—in order to make a certain section available for the six orphans and their guardian. You have never witnessed such a spirit of cooperation on the part of the passengers. We ended up having an entire section all to ourselves.

We arrived in London early in the morning. To my great surprise, we were met by a representative of the British royalty, who had been sent from Buckingham Palace to welcome the children to England. What a surprise! From London, we went by caravan 120 miles to Norwich, England, where the children's grandparents lived. The reunion was one that I shall never forget. Some of the children had never seen their grandparents before. Their grandmother had gone to great lengths to prepare their rooms and make everything ready for them. These children, who had been deprived all of their lives, suddenly found themselves in a new world of love.

The most memorable part of the trip was going to Bonds of England, one of the nation's largest department stores, and watching the children select their wardrobes. The store had invited us to arrive an hour and a half before opening hours, and they had clerks on hand to serve each of the children as they chose their clothes for the next year. All of this was paid from the funds received in America. The store cut their prices to the bone, and there were incredible bargains. It was also at a time when the dollar was very strong and could buy much more abroad. There is no way to describe the scene of these six children being given the freedom to choose whatever they wanted and needed in the way of clothing.

After a few days, I went back to London, where I had been invited to be the guest in the home of a very prominent couple who had heard about this tragic event. What royal treatment I enjoyed during the next four days. I was given a grand tour of London as few visitors ever get to see it. I wished a thousand times that Bettie had been able to accompany me on the trip. She would still be talking about it.

Because the children were American citizens and I was their legal guardian, it was compulsory that I return to England after an appointed time and affirm to the court that I was satisfied with the children's care. Of course, when I returned and saw how all of the children were loved and how well they had adjusted—some even talking in English brogue—I happily went before the court and discharged my guardianship. The funniest part was that I had to wear one of those English wigs while I was in court. I wish I had a picture of that. I didn't even get to see what I looked like in a mirror!

This was truly one of those stories that began in tragedy and then, by the grace of God and His wonderful provisions and mercy, ended well. That was 44 years ago. The sad part is that I have lost track of those precious children. However, I will always be grateful that God used me to help them through the worst time of their lives.

Chapter 12

Missions Trip to Africa

 EARLIER ON, I promised to say something about the wonderful trip and ministry experience I had while visiting the Southern Baptist mission fields in Africa. I will, after this brief detour, return to where I left off concerning my 60 years in the ministry.

From a young age, my soul yearned to be a missionary. I had a strong desire to be a missionary to the African people, and I made a strong attempt to see if I could be accepted into the field. However, because of the major health issue that occurred during my Navy days in World War II, I was told by the Foreign Mission Board of the Southern Baptist Convention that I could not be accepted for service. Despite this, God made it possible for me to visit Africa in 1967 and spend three weeks touring the mission fields in Rhodesia, Johnsonburg, and Nigeria. This made my heart burn even more to serve the Lord in that needy land.

Being a certified pilot of many years, it so happened that an organization called the Missionary Aviation Fellowship provided a Cesena aircraft and pilot to fly me, my missionary friend Bob Beaty, and other missionaries to several far-out tribes—some of whom had never seen a white person. It was a thrilling and unforgettable experience. There were two occasions on which I had the wonderful privilege of preaching to gatherings of more than 1,000 souls through several interpreters who simultaneously interpreted my sermons.

The most memorable event of the trip was a great rally that we held. Some of people from the several tribes journeyed as much as two days to get to the meeting. It turned out to be a night meeting, and the only lights were a few lanterns hanging from trees. The masses could not be seen because of the darkness, but the local missionaries estimated that well over 5,000 were in attendance.

After a long song service, I was introduced and began preaching the simplest childlike sermon you could imagine through two interpreters. I chose as my text John 3:16, and I preached for almost an hour while the interpreters relayed my sermon to that great crowd as they sat listening on the ground. They never made a sound. When I came to the invitation, Bob Beaty and the local missionaries directed the call for the lost to trust the Lord Jesus Christ. All I could do was stand and weep as I watched people begin to move forward in waves for the next 30 minutes. The missionaries who knew the local dialects dealt with people who came forward in large groups. It was past midnight when we left that glorious place where heaven had come down and filled that hallowed spot. Nothing the Lord has ever permitted me to do has moved and touched my life as much as those three weeks did in the heart of Africa.

From Rhodesia, Bulawayo, and Kenya, I went on to Nigeria, where a doctor friend of ours was serving as a dentist. While there, I saw the hand of God move in such mighty ways. I spoke at our seminary located in Ogbomosho, traveled to places where some of the most primitive tribes lived, ministered through different interpreters the good news of our Savior, and saw the working of the Holy Spirit in some of these primitive tribes.

After returning home, for weeks I experienced some of the worst nightmares you could imagine. Yet despite the poverty, squalor, disease, and death I witnessed in Africa, I still would love to have spent a lifetime ministering there. Oh, the response and affection of those wonderful souls!

Because I couldn't serve as a missionary, I promised the Lord that if He would give Bettie and me a son, I would dedicate him to be a missionary so that he might fulfill the service I was not able to fulfill. God answered our prayer, and our first child was a boy. One day, I received a phone call from Carey, our son, while he was a youth minister in Memphis. He said, "Dad, can you and Mom come over? I want to talk with you about something God is dealing with me about." We drove to Memphis, and Carey and I went for a drive. As we drove along, Carey said, "Dad, God is calling me to the mission field, and I need your blessing." At that moment, my mind rushed back to a moment in time when he was just a tiny baby. I held him in my arms and prayed that the Lord might use him some day to do a service that I wanted to do but could not because of my health. Tears filled my eyes, and I related to him the story about how I had dedicated him to serve the Lord as a missionary when he was just a tiny baby.

Bettie and I were present when Carey and Lynne were commissioned by the International Mission Board of the Southern Baptist Convention to become missionaries to Portugal. It was the fulfillment of a prayer that I shall never forget. In a way, it was as if I had gone into the mission field in the person of my precious son. My trip to Africa will live in my memory as long as I live.

Chapter 13

A New Call

EXCUSE THE DETOUR we have taken, but I wanted my mission trip experience to be injected into my memoirs. I will now return to the events that occurred during my pastorate at the First Baptist Church of Jacksonville, Arkansas.

I had invited Dr. Ramsey Pollard, the pastor of Bellevue Baptist Church in Memphis, to come and speak at a stewardship banquet as we kicked off our new financial year. When I drove him back to the airport in Little Rock, he challenged me to consider a work in Memphis in which he felt God could use me. As he painted the picture of this glowing possibility, I recall jokingly asking him, "Dr. Pollard, you aren't planning on leaving Bellevue Baptist, are you?" He assured me that he wasn't talking about his church, but rather the Wells Station Baptist Church of Memphis. He urged me and Bettie to come to Memphis, and he his and wife, Della, would show us around the city. Before he left me at the airport, he shook my hand and said, "Promise me you will think and pray about this." I said I would, and I did.

Some weeks later, Bettie and I made a drive over to Memphis, and everything we saw was appealing and intriguing. It wasn't long until a seven-member pulpit committee visited our church one Sunday morning from Wells Station. After the service, one committee member approached me and reached out his hand to introduce himself. I said, "You folks represent some church as a pulpit committee, don't you?" He smiled and asked the others to come on up. They invited us to have lunch with them. I agreed, but I suggested that we go 15 miles back to North Little Rock for more privacy. During lunch, the members described their church and dropped names of pastors whom I knew, who had sent them letters commending my ministry and the growth of the church at Jacksonville. The members strongly urged that I consider giving them a date when I would come and preach for them. I told them that it was difficult for me to even consider leaving a church where the blessings of God had been so overwhelming. On that very Sunday morning, eight souls had united with our church.

The committee members went back to Memphis, and in a few days, the telephone calls started coming. I finally agreed to come over and preach for them, but I told them that only God knew if this would be anything more than a courtesy visit. So Bettie and I went to visit the church. It was located in a blue-collar area, and its facilities were maxed out. The church was running in the 400-range in Sunday school. They needed staff and new facilities. I wasn't sure that I wanted to go into that kind of situation, because everywhere I ever pastored, including Jacksonville, we had gone through major building programs to accommodate growth. One thing I did like was that pastoring the church would give me the opportunity to again call my former associate, Mr. Charles Hill, to be my educational director and music man.

After visiting with the church and seeing the possibilities for having a great evangelistic ministry, God began to open my thinking about their challenge. We went back to Jacksonville and began praying for God's will to be done. On the one hand, we felt that there was a great opportunity to broaden our ministry to reach the masses at the air base, where some 6,000 military people were living. We had some wide-open passes there to minister as freely as we wished and bring many to Christ. But on the other hand, we were encountering some strong opposition, especially from some of the long-time senior residents who were against making the necessary changes that would be needed to make this opportunity a reality. Taking these things into consideration, I told the Lord that He would have to lead strongly and convincingly, but that I would do my best to put myself squarely into His will.

Within a short time, everything seemed to point us in the direction of being their pastor. When the church called, I felt it to be the will of God that we go to Memphis. For the third time in my ministry, I called my dear friend Charles Hill to see if God might permit him to come be my helper. Charles and Judy made a trip to Memphis, and I showed him what God had led me to do and told him that I needed his and Judy's help. They went back to Oklahoma and prayed about the challenge. God said yes, and they accepted the church's invitation to come alongside and assist me in this ministry.

Our years at Wells Station brought great joy and a wonderful harvest of souls and members by transfer of membership. It was an evangelistic field ripe for harvest. More than 800 souls came into the membership. All praise and honor be to the Lord Jesus for His mighty blessings! The Memphis area was also where our two children, Carey and

Dr. Ben Bates, Bettie Bates, Charles W, and Judy Hill

Dodie, graduated from high school. Both of them went on to the University of Tennessee at Martin, Tennessee. Carey played football on the varsity team for four years.

Following a revival in 1967 at Wells Station, Memphis, with Dr. J. Harold Smith, my associate, Mr. Charles Hill, and I baptized 122 souls in a single Sunday evening service. The closing service of that revival was held while we were still in our old auditorium, and it was packed with between 600 to 700 souls. When Dr. Smith preached his famed sermon "God's Three Deadlines," it took the better of an hour to conduct the invitation, because there was such a mass surrendering of lives to the Lord. It was a repeat of another glorious revival service we had with Dr. Smith while I was pastoring the First Baptist Church of Jacksonville, Arkansas.

Revival Crowd at Wells Station Baptist Church

Two years prior to this great outpouring in Memphis, Dr. Smith had preached a revival for us at the First Baptist Church of Jacksonville, Arkansas. That revival had also resulted in a number of souls saved and baptized. At the close of that revival, on a Sunday evening, Mr. Hill and I baptized 123 souls. Praise the Lord, on two occasions God has permitted me the overwhelming joy of participating in baptizing more than 120 souls at the close of revivals in two different churches.

Chapter 14

The End of an Era

FOLLOWING MY MINISTRY at Wells Station, I went back into full-time evangelism for a time and then took a public relations position with a church finance company located in Brentwood, Tennessee. After two years, I accepted a similar position with another church financing company in Nashville, Tennessee. I represented that company for two years, until it merged with Security Church Finance in Houston, Texas, where I served as a representative to churches for 32 years. While serving at Security Church Finance, I was transferred to Arkansas and later built a home on Petit Jean Mountain, Morrilton, Arkansas, where we lived 22 years.

My work as a consultant with Security Church Finance gave me many opportunities to preach in churches all across America and conduct a number of evangelistic meetings and Bible conferences. Without this open door to preach and minister, I could not—and would not—have continued to stay in the field of consulting. The years I spent in consulting were filled with glorious blessings too numerable to mention. There were so many doors opened to me to carry on an effective ministry, conducting Bible conferences, evangelistic crusades, soul-winning conferences, and doing interim pastoring. I was kept busy serving churches that were seeking a pastor and filling the pulpits of many churches across America.

Some of the most memorable opportunities to preach during those years came from pastors of African American churches. Life-long friendships were made, and many times I received invitations for return engagements and to conduct Bible conferences. There is no equal to the hospitality, love, and lasting friendship shown by my many black pastor friends and their congregations. Almost weekly, I receive calls and emails from beloved pastors and members of churches who just want to know how things are with me and if I am still going strong for our Lord. Of course, I happily tell them that I am still, at age 84, going at least at three-quarter speed and having the time of my life. I would rather burn out than rust out.

One of the many decisions I made that I shall always treasure was the one to go back to my native home state of Arkansas in 1977. Building a home on the beautiful Petit Jean Mountain near Morrilton, Arkansas, overlooking the winding Arkansas River, made life more than enjoyable. For 22 years we lived in the peaceable quietness of this state-park resort atmosphere. Everyone who visited the home remarked, "How did you find this piece of heaven on earth?"

I found it refreshing after so many years of being away to live within a few miles of the old home place where I grew up. There were so many memories of bygone years of sliding down the Toltec Indian Mounds on a piece of tin or getting into a large tractor tire and rolling down the Toltec mounds or taking a dare to try to swim the lake and almost losing my life. Little did we know at the time that one day an archeological discovery would be made and those very mounds on which we spent endless hours would become famous and historically important. The Arkansas Parks and Recreation Department established a beautiful state park at the Mounds site that draws visitors from every state of our country. The park is no more than three miles from where I spent my adolescent and teen years before entering the Navy during World War II.

It wasn't easy, but in 2003 I decided that, at the age of 80, it was time for me to curtail the pace of my work life, slow down the tempo, and spend more time doing some of the other things I enjoyed. Bettie and I could not imagine ever leaving our beautiful Petit Jean Mountain home and our many friends, but finally, in March 2003, we gave into the insistence of our son and daughter to move to Winter Haven, Florida. This meant moving away from friends, family, and loved ones and saying goodbye to an era of my past that is as much a part of me as life itself. It was hard to pull up stakes and move from our home, where we had lived happily for 22 years, but it had been too long since we had been able to see our children and grandchildren for longer than short, annual visits. At this stage in life, we realized that reestablishing ties with family was the most important thing we must do, so we made the move. It has been great making new friends and building a new beginning at age 84.

But did I slow down? Many of those who know me know the answer is NO, not really! Immediately after coming to Florida, I met Colonel Grady Judd of the Polk County Sheriff's Office, who at that time was campaigning to become the sheriff of Polk County. My acquaintance with Mr. Judd wasn't 10 minutes old when he challenged me to join the chaplain organization within the department. Within three weeks, I found myself being interviewed by Major Marvin

Pittman (Ret), the charge officer of the chaplains division, and then a short time later, sworn in as a sheriff's chaplain. Now I am part of a group of active chaplains who serve in many ministry capacities on a "volunteer basis" and are on call "24-7."

Dr. Ben in Chaplain Uniform

In order to establish myself in Florida, information of my move was sent to some 150 Baptist churches within a radius of 35 miles of my new home. Soon, doors began to open, and opportunities to serve as a supply speaker for pastors who had to be away from their pulpits and invitations to conduct evangelistic crusades began coming in. Before I knew it, pastors were calling more and more. I was beginning to get back to preaching the good news of the Word of God Sunday after Sunday.

There were a few roadblocks that set me back in 2006 and 2007. In 2006, I underwent major back surgery, and the screws and steel rods that were put into my back during the procedure slowed me down for four weeks. The first time back in the pulpit, I had to wear a bulky back and chest brace. But five minutes after stepping into the pulpit, I forgot everything but what I love to do. I even carried along a stool but forgot to use it. Again in 2006, four months following the back surgery, I had a partial knee replacement. By the grace of God, I was back preaching three weeks later. That knee operation was a failure, and I had to go for a full knee replacement on the same knee in 2007. This time, I was down for four weeks.

Many of my dear friends would ask me how I could do it. All I could say was, "The love I have for what God gifted and called me to do always gives me the strength. If there is pain, I overlook it, and God makes up the difference." During those times of my recovery, I thought much about the awful pain our Lord endured as they beat Him with their fists, whipped Him with a whip, and made Him carry His cross up the hill to Calvary. I thought about how they forced Him down upon that cross, drove spikes through his pain-jerked body, lifted Him between heaven and hell, and then dropped the cross into the socket. I thought about His mangled body and how He agonized for six horrible hours until He finally said, "It is finished." What my Lord bore in His body on the tree made what I was going through seem as nothing.

Many have been the times that someone has asked me, "Preacher, as you look back over the last 60 years, do you have any regrets?" Of course, there are many things I would have done differently. Most of us would change some of the things in our past if it were possible. I deeply regret the wasted years of my early life. But over all, I am pleased to leave it all in the hands of a gracious and merciful God, who does all things well.

It has been such a great joy and privilege to recall the memories of a lifetime and share them with whomever may read these memoirs. Along the way, through these 60 years, I have met thousands of people with whom it has been my great joy to share the good news of our Savior. God permitted me the great honor of being the pastor of some of the finest and most caring people on the face of the earth. It will be a glorious day when this life is over and my work here on earth is complete and I hear my Lord say, "Come on home, Ben. Your loved ones and those precious souls on whom you had an influence to take me as their Savior are waiting to welcome you home."

Thank you for reading my "memoirs." It is my earnest prayer that you *personally* know the Lord Jesus Christ in an experiential way as your Lord and Savior. To just know about Him is not enough. Jesus Christ was crucified on a Roman cross and buried in a tomb, but three days later, He rose from the dead. He ascended back to the Father and is going to return some day to this earth. Dear friend, if you believe with all your heart what you just read and you simply ask Christ to make you His own child by faith, He will make you a part of the family of God, and one day, I will meet you in heaven. Thank you, Lord Jesus!

Ben Bates, D.D.
Winter Haven, Florida

Printed in the United States
143181LV00001B/10/P